Pulpit, Pew, and Politics

by

James I. Spainhower

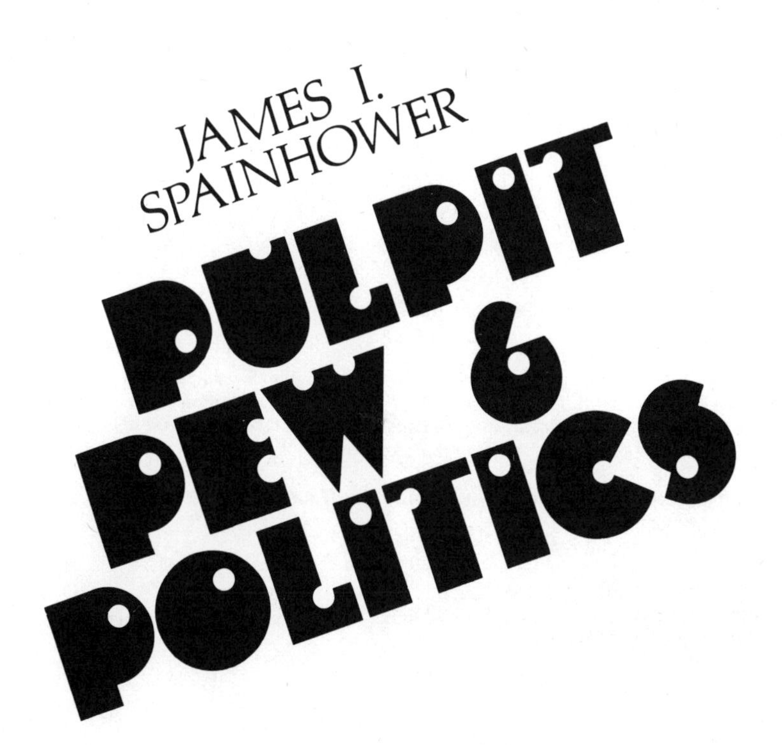

The Bethany Press
St. Louis, Mo.

Library of Congress Cataloging in Publication Data
Spainhower, James I
Pulpit, pew, and politics.

1. Christianity and politics. I. Title.
BR115.P7S638 261.7 79-12855
ISBN 0-8272-2926-7

Printed in the United States of America
Distributed in Canada by G. R. Welch Co. Ltd., Toronto.

Dedicated
to
The Three J's
Joanne Janet Jeff

Contents

James Spainhower and his family.

Acknowledgments

Through the years my thinking has been enriched greatly by countless writers, political speakers, clergy friends and associates in the world of politics and government and in the world of religion. The Endnotes at the back of the book give credit to those I have quoted directly. To others, including the parishioners of congregations I have served as pastor, and constituents I have served as an elected official, my debt is immense. They have compelled me by their spiritual and political requirements to reflect on the meaning of service in both areas.

There are some who deserve a special word of thanks. My secretary of over sixteen years, Mrs. Georgia Schulte, has given literally hundreds of hours to this book's preparation. I shall never cease to be amazed at her steadiness under pressure. Sherman Hanson, Editor of The Bethany Press, encouraged me to write this book and provided sound advice in the process of its completion. My friend of many years, Guin Tuckett, a Vice President of the Christian Board of Publication, and in charge of product development and design was helpful in the final stages of the book's production. Jake Wolf, a former reporter for the *St. Louis Post-Dispatch* and my press secretary, read and assisted in numerous revisions of the manuscript. My personal assistant, Robert Jordan, offered creative suggestions at many points. Howard E. Short, my former seminary professor and a former editor for Bethany Press and *The Christian* magazine, gave valuable counsel on numerous occasions.

My thanks to each of these, none of whom can be faulted for the book's deficiencies but each of whom deserves credit for any value the book might possess.

Finally, to my wife Joanne, my daughter Janet, and my son Jeff, who through the years have shared more than any family should have to share, the time and person of a husband and father, I gratefully dedicate this book.

James I. Spainhower
Jefferson City, Missouri
August, 1979

Prologue

This is a book about religion and politics.

It is important for the reader to know at the beginning that I am a member of the Christian faith and of the Democratic party. I declare my religious and political membership in neither a spirit of pride nor by way of apology but only to help the reader better understand and interpret the views expressed.

A further explanation is necessary. Although I am a Christian, I do not believe all religious truth is confined to the Christian faith. Jesus did say he came to reveal the way, the truth, and the life but he did not claim his to be the only way, the only truth, and the only life. I am convinced that Jesus' life and words emphasize the truth about God in whatever religious garment it may be clothed.

I have been blessed with the friendship of many persons of the Jewish faith and impressed by their personal dedication to the same principles of truth, honor, and justice that my Christian faith has taught me to uphold. I know we worship the same God.

And although a lifelong Democrat, I know that all political wisdom is not confined to my party. I admire the Democratic party for its record of policy-making on behalf of the underprivileged and needy, but I also admit that there have been periods in this nation's history when other parties have better served them.

Membership in a political party does not require unreasonable partisanship. Nor does it necessitate unthinking, blind loyalty to every position a party takes. Parties themselves are so contradictory that the member who insists on following its dictates without raising questions is certain to end up as a fool. One of the chief ways that parties are disciplined, other than by losing elections, is from challenges in its own ranks to party positions. Also, positions taken by a party in one period of history may drastically change with the passage of years. Further, political parties in one section of the country may vary greatly in their attitudes from political parties in other parts of the country.

I stress these points because it is necessary to guard against making an ideological god out of one's political party affiliation. A political party is merely an instrument, although a very important instrument, for influencing political decisions.

Individuals who would attempt to transfer the power of personal religious beliefs to the unwieldy representation of the many voices which speak in a political party will encounter difficulty. I personally identify with the point made in a *Wall Street Journal* editorial that quests for high ethical standards in politics not only attract public admiration and support "but they can also bring embarrassment and confusion when the compromises of politics and the imperfections of men and institutions come inevitably to public light."[1] These words echo clearly the reaction heard so often from the average citizen: "I've known too many politicians who were supposed to have high morals but turned out to be run-of-the-mill once they got into office."

But all human beings, whether political or non-political, are fallible. Even the most saintly experience spiritual inadequacy. Those who think the art of government can be practiced on a purely spiritual plane are skating on thin ice. As that *Wall Street Journal* editorial puts it, ". . . when policies go awry, bringing real threats to the security of the people and genuine hardships to their daily lives, ethical leadership will sound more and more like mere posturing."[2] The mouthing of high ideals is never a worthy substitute for economic growth, sound money, peace, security, and those other evidences of the presence of an enlightened public policy.

Consequently, as I emphasize the need for ethical and moral guideposts in politics, at the same time I recognize substantive policies must be socially and technically sound. Religious conscience is needed in government, but it can never be substituted for political service and competence. Government invites social disruption when it neglects the development and implementation of sound and sensible public policies.

Any government, though, that does not consider the moral and ethical implications of policy-making will soon face a disturbing spiritual crisis among those who are governed.

No city, county, state, or nation will remain stable for long if ill-served ethically or politically by government.

I strongly believe that too little emphasis has been placed on the role of religion in providing the ethical ingredient needed to complement political expertise in a well-governed society.

That is why this book has been written.

1

A Smile or a Scowl? —The Mixing of Religion and Politics

In the winter of 1962 I announced my intention to file for public office. A few days later I met on the street a parishioner of the church of which I was pastor. I greeted him warmly, only to see his face break out, not with his usual smile but with a scowl. He did not respond with customary friendly words but instead growled, "Hello, politician."

My friend was not pleased that I intended to devote part of my time to being a politician. He, like millions of persons, holds politics and politicians in low esteem. Shakespeare's observation that a politician is "one that would circumvent God"[3] reflects their views perfectly. They refuse to participate in politics and have no respect for those who do. Politics and politicians prompt their scowls, not their smiles!

Although persons with such extreme, negative views are a minority, the moderate views of politics and politicians held by the majority are not much more encouraging. The reluctance of citizens to become politically involved is widespread—many even refuse to vote. This tendency of millions of people to disdain participation in politics is alarming.

Those who treat politics and politicians with low regard or contempt offer many reasons for doing so.

"What's the use of taking part in politics?" some ask. "You really can't accomplish anything." They perceive politics as a futile activity but are willing to be involved in public causes regarded as more productive and attractive.

"Politics is so confusing," claim others. They are perplexed by the number and complexity of decisions that confront politicians. The contradictory views expressed by opposing parties and, at times, by members of the same party, jumble public issues together and form a quagmire for many persons. They flee from any opportunity to assist in bringing order to chaos in government.

"I can't afford to get involved in politics," is another reason frequently advanced for antipathy. This attitude reflects caution, or perhaps even fright, of the delicate and sensitive matters with which the public expects politics and politicians to deal. Citizens in business or the professions, who depend on public goodwill for success and profit, fear offending potential customers and clients.

"Politics will alienate your friends," some objectors say. They avoid the political arena for fear of fracturing social relationships. They are afraid friendship cannot be maintained between persons on the opposite sides of issues.

"I don't have time for politics" is a reason voiced occasionally. There is so much to do and many activities are more appealing than political involvement. Good can be accomplished by participation in less controversial endeavors. Then, too, time given to politics as a volunteer is lost to hobbies, moments of leisure and recreation and family activities.

Each of the reasons cited is valid under certain conditions.

But one reason frequently given simply is not true: "It is morally wrong to participate in politics." Those who refrain from political activity know that politics involves the resolution of conflicting opinions of persons and groups who seek a public policy which each person and group can accept. These critics insist that political activity is morally questionable because compromise of basic principles is necessary to produce agreement.

It is wrong, they say, because principles ought to reflect a person's basic faith as to how the God he worships would have him live. God can never smile on persons or groups who compromise his principles.

But analysis of this position reveals two unwarranted assumptions. First, how can any moral person or group presume to know *for certain* what are God's principles? Second, even if there is general agreement among most persons and societies as to the basic nature of God's principles, human nature assures there will always be ethical failures.

No one is perfect except God, so what is unusual about the necessity for compromise in politics? Principles are compromised in all moral endeavors. A politician must exercise common sense. He must develop the capacity to distinguish between compromises that are acceptable and productive and others that are unacceptable or even dishonest.

The feeling that something is innately wrong about participating in politics especially pervades the thinking of religiously sensitive Americans. It is the premise of this book that politics is appropriate for their participation and that God wants his children to be involved. And persons who become active in politics, whether on a volunteer or full-time basis, are politicians!

I insist, simply, God knows and cares about politicians too! He does not scowl; he smiles on politicians. He desires and needs their service to his children as much as he desires and needs the service of businessmen, farmers, homemakers, students, ministers, teachers, laborers, and all other persons, regardless of vocation.

God knows politicians, but do they know God? Some do and some do not. The more politicians who do know God, the greater the promise of enlightened and morally sound public policies.

If God knows politicians and approves of their presence in his world, he surely must expect their conduct to be in accord with his wishes. Simply stated, God expects politicians to devise policies that will help, rather than hinder the efforts of citizens to lead godly lives.

There are good persons and bad persons in all areas of life. When good things happen and moral deeds and godly acts occur in government, it is partly the result of politicians who are sensitive to the overreaching purposes of God for all mankind. The possibility of good public policy is enhanced when politicians are willing to mix religion and politics in a responsible manner.

But, mankind has been told for years that religion and politics don't mix. In my life I have heard that cliché repeated as if it were holy writ in sacred books of the great religions of the world. To accept that cliché is to exclude politics and politicians from the presence of God.

This book, therefore, holds that religion and politics do mix. It does not argue by recourse to theology and political philosophy. Those who seek such arguments for mixing religion and politics are advised to look elsewhere. There are numerous books available for the reader who wishes to explore the theological and philosophical bases for blending religion and politics. Many of Reinhold Niebuhr's writings deal forthrightly with the theological aspects, especially *Moral Man and Immoral Society*. Thomas G. Sanders' *Protestant Concepts of Church and State* is an excellent survey of institutional relationships between church and state. A brief but lucid and theologically oriented presentation is found in William Lee Miller's *The Protestant and Politics*.

My premise is that religion and politics have been intertwined since the beginning of human civilization and will remain so as long as there is a human race. We may or may not approve of how this occurs, but that it does occur cannot be denied by an objective reading of history. Historical works such as Arnold Toynbee's *A Study of History* or the writings of Will Durant provide ample illustration of the intertwining of religious and political concerns in nearly all cultures throughout recorded history. The Hebrew heritage is a classic example of the almost total union in the nation's life of its religious beliefs and political practices.

Religion and politics always will be mixed because there is a spiritual and social need for them. Regardless of an individual's degree of intellect, whether it be a mind of simplicity, of average endowment or brilliance, all must deal with the gift of life in terms of a personal faith and spend their days among contemporaries under the guidance of that faith. To find that faith involves a personal religious quest; being a member of a governed society thrusts a person into political activities.

Although combining religion and politics may be inevitable, the actual mixing of the two is another matter. Some persons have so little regard for both that they refuse to learn the meaning of either.

Others contend that religion is more important than politics because it considers questions of the origin and destiny of persons. Consequently, temporal matters are dismissed as unworthy of consideration.

The solely politically-minded admit ignorance of our origin and destiny; they believe that enlightenment on those subjects is impossible. However, they insist that the recurring difficulties we human beings have experienced in living together are amenable to purely secular resolution, and deserve careful attention from us all.

But there is a breed of citizens who take issue with the narrowness of such opinions. Their enlightened life-style includes both religion and politics for an active, purposeful existence.

They are willing to share their faith but refuse to force it on anyone because they recognize that a personal faith is always chosen freely.

They accept as inevitable that they will exist in the presence of those who do not share their faith but whom they must respect if everyone is to live in peace.

They believe there is a good chance that people may live in harmony and peace if guided by sincerity in deciding the rules that will govern their lives together.

They become involved in politics because they feel that the political realm is an area of life where personal faith must be tested.

Their personal faith may be challenged by participating in politics, but they believe that when faith is tempered by such an experience, its true strength will be measured.

I have concluded that there are many persons who desire to become politicians of this type. They strongly believe religion and politics should be mixed, but they do not know how. This book tries to provide practical guidance for them.

I recognize that any art, even the art of mixing religion and politics, reaches greatest perfection when mastered so completely that it can be performed almost effortlessly.

My mother was an expert gardener who each summer cultivated one of the most productive vegetable plots grown in our hometown of Stanberry. I can see her now, standing ankle deep in freshly plowed soil, planting a crop that would receive her attentive care.

Her specialty was green peas, which flourished in the cooler temperatures of the early growing season that prevails in Gentry County in the northwest section of Missouri.

One of my favorite boyhood activities was to break open the newly harvested pods and carefully inspect the uniform row of tender young peas that a miracle of God had left inside. Those little green morsels had a world of their own within their pod.

Religion and politics are like peas, existing side by side in a pod that is their world. They wait there to provide spiritual nourishment and social enlightenment for whoever avails themselves of their riches.

I have learned that both nourishment and enlightenment are received by those who are concerned with religion and politics.

There were many opportunities in my formative years to view the mixing of religion and politics from close quarters. Discussions of those two topics were frequent in our home. These discussions often developed into rather loud and exciting arguments, which made them even more interesting to me, youngest of fourteen children. Thus, early in life I became fascinated with the contrasts, the emotional impact, and the raw appeal of religion and politics.

Because my family was poor, I became well informed about government relief programs in my early years. Before the Great Depression, my parents accumulated substantial wealth from farming. They lost everything after 1929, and my father was forced to work for the WPA. He was issued what he called "Roosevelt overalls" and detested wearing them. Commodity food was eaten at our house, and two of my brothers went to CCC camps, the Civilian Conservation Corps established by Roosevelt. They helped support the family on the $25 a month which the government sent home for each of them.

Unfortunately, my parents separated when I was eight years old, apparently because of the strains and hardships of those terrible years. I then became a welfare child and benefitted from government payments made to my mother, who cared for the five children still at home attending grade school. As a result of this vivid childhood experience, I can testify that my family would have suffered even worse hardship had it not been for the governmental relief programs designed by the New Deal to meet the desperate economic needs of helpless citizens.

My mother always insisted that people will do good for others, especially for the poor, when their values are molded by religion. She also believed that the basis for many of the political activities of the New Deal was rooted in a religiously-oriented idealism.

This strong parental influence heightened my interest in politics and, as a high school student in the early 1940s, I became fascinated with the political abilities of President Franklin D. Roosevelt. My mother's near worship of FDR, contrasted with my father's near hatred of him, made FDR's leadership even more enticing to a teenager making his first political judgments.

This family portrait, taken in 1932, shows the author when he was four years old. The youngest child in a family of 14, he is standing with his hand on his mother's chair. Two children, not shown, died in infancy.

During my senior year of high school in 1946, my church sent me to Washington, D. C., to attend a political education seminar on postwar problems. I was confronted there with an appeal for the application of my religious faith to political problems whose solution had been postponed during World War II. One of the most urgent was the denial of basic human rights to black Americans.

In those early postwar days, prejudice against blacks was widespread, and full civil rights existed only in a few states. Through the prodding of Eleanor Roosevelt and others, the nation was forced to face the terrible injustices perpetrated against blacks. But Congress could not be persuaded to enact the constitutional guarantees of equality into Federal law (and did not do so until 1957).

I can recall my dismay, as I sat in the gallery of the U. S. Senate, to hear the words of bias and prejudice uttered on the floor below by Senator Theodore Bilbo of Mississippi. My young mind instantly knew that the enactment of just laws could be impeded by the absence of the human values nurtured by religion.

As a college student in Oklahoma during the late forties, and as a seminary student in Kentucky during the final years of President Harry S Truman's administration, both my studies and current events convinced me of an inevitable intertwining of religious and political concerns. Those were days when many persons, whose religious idealism molded their social concerns, were activists seeking to stop the spread of atomic weapons. They did their utmost to promote the peaceful utilization of nuclear power. It was difficult for them to understand how truly religious persons could refuse to become involved in a grass-roots political movement dedicated to preventing a nuclear holocaust. They believed it was self-evident that a person's religious ideals compel that person to be active politically.

With the seeds of protest movements sprouting throughout the nation, I began my career as a clergyman in Arkansas in 1953 during the governorship of Orval Faubus and the presidency of Dwight D. Eisenhower. My initial ministry, at the First Christian Church in Fayetteville, was a casualty of the racial turmoil in Arkansas, whose citizens were roused to the hottest anger as they rallied in support of Faubus' defiance of Federal troops at Central High School in Little Rock. When I received a black college student into the membership of my all-white congregation, a group of parishioners immediately moved to amend our church's constitution to forbid membership to any non-Caucasian. Other members of the congregation, to their credit, defeated the amendment, but my ministry was seriously weakened. I knew I should move on, and within a year I accepted the pastorate of a church at Marshall, Missouri.

Four years later, in 1962, I made a major decision in my life. I decided to combine my profession as a clergyman with a career as a politician. I became a candidate for state representative from Saline County to the Missouri General Assembly.

The sanctuary was completely filled on the cold Sunday morning in February when I announced my decision to parishioners. I was nervous, even though the general board of the church had met four days before and approved my decision by a vote of 30 to 3.

In explaining to my congregation why I was seeking election to a public office, I said: "The more I observe the condition of our social order and the tremendous problems that confront people daily—the more conscious I become of the vital role of politics and government in molding the social order and in helping or hindering persons from facing up to their full potential. Many areas of our lives are regulated by government—sometimes rightly so and at other times unrightly so. Many of the services upon which people depend—mental health facilities, law enforcement, and social welfare, to mention a few—are controlled by the processes of government. Many of our human rights, which are of paramount importance to the free function of religion, are subject to the whims of government. Civil rights, political and religious freedom, the separation of church and state, and the freedom to think and speak as we feel led by our conscience—the continuance of these are largely dependent upon decisions made in the governmental realm.

"Consequently, I have felt a growing concern that government be moral and ethical, for unless it is this, it will ultimately fail to be of genuine service to God and mankind. As a Christian, I believe these moral and ethical principles are most clearly revealed in the Christian faith, and the insights of this faith need to be brought to the making of our laws. Therefore, I feel that the concerns, attitudes, and insights—not only of lawyers, merchants, farmers, and educators but also those trained to look at things from the moral and ethical perspective—must be brought to the tasks of government. This is the basic orientation of a minister's training. A minister is taught to ask: 'What is the will of God in this particular situation?'

"In the light of these facts, I keep asking myself: 'Wouldn't it be good—helpful—if there were persons here and there in government who are trained in seeking moral and ethical answers as well as those whose primary training has been in law, economics, or political science?' The conclusion I keep coming back to is: 'Yes, there is a place and a need for such persons—and maybe this is what God wants me to try to do.' I have therefore decided that I must seek some manner of more adequately expressing the convictions I feel about these matters."

I did not fully realize then that I would become as involved in politics and government as I have. Nor did I recognize how inadequate are good intentions and high ideals by themselves in the fascinating but complicated world of politics and government.

The words I spoke with such fervor in the early sixties now disturb me with two rather easy assumptions that are implied: A man *can* determine what is "right," what is the will of God in a particular situation; and he can make those evaluations as a "man of God" who is, in my words on that Sunday morning, "trained to look at things from the moral and ethical perspective."

Through the years I have become less and less certain that my specific views can be paralleled with the will of God or even with what is "right" in a particular situation. I always *hope* my views are in accord with those of the Eternal, but specific instances are fewer and fewer when I can exclaim with dogmatic emphasis, "This is what is right, for this is the will of God!"

Frankly, whenever any person says he is doing something because God told him to, I begin to wonder why God told him while keeping so many others ignorant. The individual who claims to have a divine patent on what is "right" has the makings of a dangerous demagogue, whether in politics or any other area of life. Americans are basically a religious people, and anyone who convincingly speaks of knowing what is "right" can get the ear of many people. The intoxication of public attention makes otherwise sane and sensible persons drunk with delusions of their own capacity to speak "the truth" unerringly. The insidious temptation to play the role of a minor god and define what is right lurks in the halls of government for many well-intentioned persons who become involved in politics.

Soon after my election to the Missouri House of Representatives I recognized that it is not always possible to know what is right when confronted with a difficult public issue. I realized that legislative decision-making requires technical competence and a thorough understanding of how politics and government operate. My woeful deficiency in political science, constitutional theory, parliamentary procedures and intergovernmental relations became personally bothersome. It was very difficult to deal intelligently with a multitude of substantive issues because I lacked knowledge and was unprepared to render the moral and ethical judgments I had thought would be so simple to proclaim.

The only solution to this problem was to return to school for more training. I chose political science as my field of study and was gratified for the assistance it gave to my political and governmental activities.

A
MAN
ALL

But there was an added increment I had not expected. In studying political theory, I was compelled to grapple with theological, ethical, and moral questions in a far broader social context than I had twenty years earlier as a seminary student. Or maybe it was just that my interests had become more socially oriented.

Whatever the reason, a return to a study of seminary subjects like the nature of humankind, the nature of society, the origin of ideas of right and wrong, and the fundamental concepts of various forms of government was welcome. Aristotle, Plato, Thomas Jefferson, Reinhold Niebuhr, Paul Tillich, John Stuart Mill, Francis Bacon, Rousseau, John Locke, Karl Marx, and other thinkers were revisited. Their views took on new meaning and relevance for the hard-core issues of life. The mixing of religion and politics through the ages became more real than ever before. I realized that my efforts to become politically proficient were forcing me to grasp for answers that have been the elusive object of humanity's mental and spiritual inquiry since the beginning of time.

As a result of those six years of graduate study in political science, combined with my continuing ministry in the church and service in the Missouri House of Representatives, my basic view that the mixing of religion and politics has always existed was reinforced. My conviction that high ideals must motivate and guide the activities of those involved in politics was also strengthened.

Unfortunately, I found that many in political life view high ideals as did the philosopher Francis Bacon. Bacon contended that high ideals are like the stars, ". . . which give little light because they are so high." Respectfully, I would question Bacon's conclusion. Any Boy Scout knows that someone lost in a wilderness of trees, snow, or sand may find his way to safety by following the stars. It is more than a beautiful story that the three wise men in the familiar Christmas story were led to a greater source of wisdom because they followed the glimmering light of the star in the East.

In the fifteenth century there lived in Europe a political scientist by the name of Machiavelli who shared Bacon's distrust of idealism. He became a persuasive advocate of utilitarianism, of practicality, which states that the ends justify any means. The "Machiavellian" approach to politics and government has come to be labeled as any political method devoid of basic virtues. Its advocates are willing to adopt any method, ethical or not, to achieve success. Machiavelli broke with the political philosophies of Plato and Aristotle, ethical giants who reasoned that people, seeing what was highest, might lead better lives. These philosophers believed that if persons did not see the highest, their reach would inevitably be shortened.

Machiavelli responded that the classical philosophers would have persons reach beyond their capacity for achievement and, becoming discouraged at failing to achieve such high goals, would give up. Machiavelli provided lower goals. He lowered life standards so people might more easily achieve them.

Many in public life seek to do this. They lower the standards for the operation of government and for the daily execution of its business. They claim too much is expected of mere human beings. They appeal to the animal instincts of people and disregard the ageless teachings of the classics, of the Jewish and Moslem faiths, and of the Christian belief that individuals are more than animals. They forget or do not believe that people are creatures of God, created only a little lower than the angels. They do not realize that the real tragedy is not that we aim too high but that we aim too low. They are unaware that the trouble is not that too much is expected of us, but too little. We were never meant to be animals; we have a touch of the eternal in us—an essential divine decency that we cannot disregard if we expect to gain true satisfaction from living. Human existence is that sense of the divine mixed with the substance of earthly life.

2

What Religion and Politics Are All About

At least three problems confront those who would mix religion and politics: The lack of understanding of religion, the failure to grasp the function and purpose of politics in resolving conflicting opinions and goals, and the refusal to accept the limitations of both religion and politics. It is essential to conquer these three difficult problems if the scope of religion and politics is to be fully realized.

What Religion is About

Much of the negative criticism of religion is nonsense.

Adult rejection of formal affiliation with a religious denomination often is the result of an experience at an earlier age involving a sternly issued demand for religious commitment that was not always clearly understood by a child or adolescent. These individuals, unfortunately, tend to banish religion forever from their thoughts and activities.

There are also those whose religious tolerance is so limited that they are angered when a believer publicly affirms religious faith. I once found myself the target of such abuse in a disagreeable encounter with an elderly man in Miami Beach. He stopped me on the street after noticing the convention badge I wore, which indicated that I was a delegate to the annual national convention of my church. He glared at me, blurting out, "I've got no use for the church or anything else religious."

I did not realize then, of course, that my later career in religion and politics would not come full circle with intolerance until that unforgettable encounter with a parishioner who greeted me with a scowl and said, "Hello, politician."

President Harry S Truman, a powerful leader with deeply religious beliefs, demonstrated suspicion and impatience with those who publicly profess their faith. He told a biographer, Merle Miller, that his Grandfather Young felt the same way. He recalled a church in the front yard of his country home that the Baptists and Methodists and others used. When Truman was six years old, his grandfather told him that "whenever the customers in any of those denominations prayed too loud in the Amen corner, you'd better go home and lock your smokehouse." Truman confessed he had found that to be true. "I've never cared much for the loud pray-ers or for people who do that much going on about religion," the fiery President told Miller.[4]

Too many persons, unfortunately, dwell on similar memories and experiences which cause them to reason that religion is counterfeit. They let a bias incubated in childhood serve as the foundation for adult views. The wisdom expressed by U. S. Supreme Court Justice Robert H. Jackson in the 1948 McCollum case escapes them. He wrote: "The fact is that, for good or for ill, nearly everything in our culture worth transmitting, everything which gives meaning to life, is saturated with religious influences, derived from paganism, Judaism, Christianity—both Catholic and Protestant — and other faiths accepted by a large part of the world's peoples."[5]

Those words are strong reminders that religion is too vital to permit negative impressions or bias from childhood to impede its role in life. All of us must understand what religion is about and its importance to us!

Persons are motivated by what they really believe, by their personal religious faith. Religion is, as the theologian Paul Tillich defined it, "ultimate concern." Whatever is done with a life will express what is, for that person, of ultimate concern. Try as we may, we cannot escape the truth that every person has a God in whom to believe, and one always winds up giving spiritual allegiance to that God. Because human beings are of the flesh and of the earth, that allegiance must be expressed through human means in an earthly environment. Heaven may be our ultimate goal, but first we must contend with the here and now.

To go one step further, religion has to do with a human view, here and now, as to our origin in days past and our destiny in days to come. These religious opinions must be formulated because what happens between our origin and destiny will be determined largely by our opinion as to our origin and destiny.

An astounding number of persons in every generation are uncomfortable searching for our origin and destiny. They feel that the attainment of such knowledge is beyond our human capacity. Others, with whose views I am in accord, believe but cannot test-tube prove, that our origin is of an ultimate being most call God, and that our destiny lies with this same God.

Bernard M. G. Reardon, an Englishman who isolated the superhuman aspect of religion, once said that "religion springs up as faith in superhuman spiritual powers, by whose help the power which man possesses of himself is in some way supplemented and elevated . . . a match for the pressure of the natural world." [6] This kind of language frightens some people and is considered poppycock by many who believe they are more sophisticated. But Reardon is correct in his judgment of what religion is about—faith in a God whose divine power is available to help us face problems which confront us in *this* world.

Religion is not *first* a doctrinal expression or a worship experience. *First* it is the feeling, the conviction, the frightening awareness that life is too much for us alone—we must have help from God.

My personal pilgrimage of faith has been greatly aided by the writings of Harry Emerson Fosdick. His observation that "men never really find God until they need him" has certainly proved true in my own life. It has been in circumstances of critical personal need and frustration that I have had my most meaningful encounters with God. Until there occurs some almost devastating experience through which the relevance of faith in God is clearly demonstrated, many persons never recognize that their religion must reflect their everyday life, or it really is not true religion.

Religion as a Way of Faith

Of bedrock concern in determining a person's way of faith is what one believes is most important for one's life. A distinction should be made between what is rationally *known* to be most important and what is *believed* to be most important. What a person believes is most important is what a person actually desires to come to pass.

A meaningful faith confronts persons daily with moral and ethical choices as to what is really most important in their lives. What people believe is reflected in the morality of their actions. The superiority of religious values for our life in this world is demonstrated in our capacity to produce what most neutral observers agree is good. Admittedly, there are instances when values, whose origin can be traced to religion, have bad consequences for people, but these are exceptions.

For most persons, what they believe is most important is what they conclude is truly good for them and all others.

John W. Gardner, the first Secretary of the Department of Health, Education, and Welfare and the founder of the citizen's lobby, Common Cause, voiced an idea in the sixties which probably reflects the religious views of many. "I believe," he wrote, "that most Americans would welcome a new burst of moral commitment and an end to the apathy, indifference, and disengagement which have crept over the nation." [7] Gardner contends that people would rather work hard for something they believe in than enjoy a pampered idleness, and would rather give up their comfort for an honored objective than bask in extravagant leisure.

The quest for a just society in which the ethical ideal is a guiding force must spring from persons of religious faith, because the evidence is clear that rational thought alone will not produce the ordered society.

Show-Me State citizens and others who require further explanation of the foregoing statement may consider the words of Reinhold Niebuhr, a native Missourian described by the Encyclopedia Americana as ". . . the most notable American-born Protestant theologian of the twentieth century."

In 1932, he said, "The growing intelligence of mankind seems not to be growing rapidly enough to achieve mastery over the social problems, which the advances of technology create." [8] And, he added, "Without the ultrarational hopes and passions of religion no society will ever have the courage to conquer despair and attempt the impossible; . . ."[9]

Niebuhr was born June 21, 1892, in Wright City, Missouri, and was reared in that small farming community, where his father was pastor of the Evangelical Synod Church. This brilliant super-achiever taught in New York City at the famed Union Theological Seminary and was an activist in partisan politics. He took the side of workers in the early years of the labor movement and was a spokesman for liberal positions in both the Liberal and Democratic parties. National leaders repeatedly asked his counsel on issues.

He died in 1971, leaving an extraordinary record in blending religion and politics. He explained well the need for religion as a way of faith. But Niebuhr and others also recognize that religion is more than faith—it is life itself!

Religion as a Way of Life

If the object of faith is that which is considered to be truly important, then religion determines the way life is lived. The substance of faith is the narrows within whose confines moves the current of life. Religious values are powerful determinants of personal actions and of the way of life a nation follows.

The importance of religion in the American way of life has been emphasized by nearly every great American leader since the birth of our nation.

In his farewell address, George Washington observed: "Of all the dispositions and habits which lead to political prosperity, religion and morality are indispensable supports." He also issued a warning that all generations of Americans should heed: "And let us with caution indulge the supposition that morality can be maintained without religion."

In more recent times the inaugural address of John F. Kennedy is a masterpiece of political expression based on the abiding religious values of America.

Kennedy closed his inaugural address with one of the finest appeals in American history for Americans to seek the guidance of God: "With a good conscience our only sure reward, with history the final judge of our deeds, let us go forth to lead the land we love, asking His blessing and His help, but knowing that here on earth God's work must truly be our own."

Carved in stone on a wall of the Senate chamber in the Missouri Capitol are the words of the nineteenth century statesman of Ireland, Daniel O'Connell: "Nothing can be politically right that is morally wrong." This surely must be the conviction of every deeply religious person. In politics, or in business, or in marital relations, or in labor-management relations—anywhere persons are found living out their days, that which is moral, ethical, "right"—ultimately makes the best sense as a preferred way of life.

Even the religious cynic Sigmund Freud admitted that whether religious or philosophical systems are conceived as the highest achievement of the human, or deplored as fallacies, it must be acknowledged that where they exist, and especially where they are on the rise, they testify to a high level of civilization. Freud's argument is simply that a civilization's way of life is molded by the way of life of its citizens, and the way of life of its citizens is given form and shape by their religion.

The modern tendency to divide the religious from the secular will fail simply because absolute separation is neither desirable nor possible. Actually, absolute distinction between the sacred and the secular is not even acceptable to most religions. The historic religions generally find hints of what eternity holds for us in the clay of this world. Real religious experiences usually do not grow out of speculative curiosity about the world and its constitution, but from the situations in which we actually find ourselves.

As we examine the situation in which we find ourselves and evaluate our personal way of life and the way of life followed by those about us, we probably do not like what we see. The crime, the drug addiction, the wars, the poverty . . . these defects in our life together are glaring. It is apparent that the primary values of the world's religions have not been adopted by enough persons as the norm for individual and corporate ways of life.

The presence of persons in places of public leadership who are religiously ignorant, ethically amoral, and spiritually impoverished provide sufficient evidence against the call for more secularization. Pathological attempts to religionize the secularity of today are certain to fail. Instead there must be people and institutions making extraordinary efforts to cultivate personal and corporate consciences to respond to the high ethical and moral principles of the great religions of the world. There must be a dramatic increase in the number of persons willing to have their religious faith determine the values by which they live.

Today, millions of Americans are fleeing from religious faith because they see no permanent remedy in religion for their personal and collective inability to cope with the dizzying acceleration of change in their midst. This contemporary flight from religion, when what is needed personally and socially is something solid, something permanent on which to depend, is a modern tragedy.

Salvation from this unmanageable quicksand culture will be possible only if religious faith is the foundation on which lives are built. Tinkering with shallow answers to the serious problems of twentieth century existence will not suffice. Nothing except solid religious faith will show the way to social order and peace of mind.

I once read an article that portrayed faith as a fleeing to religion for protection from the hard realities of life. Some do view religion as a cave to hide in from the potential blasts of life. But that is neither an accurate nor mature view of religion.

A concept of religion that causes a person to retreat from intellectual confrontations with what life is all about is inadequate. Religion that influences a person to deny objective truth is invalid. Religion that puts one down instead of elevating one to a position just a little lower than the Creator is questionable.

True religion creates pride in persons as God's creations in his image. True religion evokes humility that recognizes as foolish all who think we can understand completely our beginnings and describe perfectly our destiny.

The philosopher Whitehead once observed that religion is what a person does with his solitariness. Reinhold Niebuhr put it another way when he contended that human beings are incurably religious.

In 1939 my mother and two of my sisters were given a trip to the New York World's Fair by our family's "rich aunt." (To a family on welfare, this school-teacher aunt was rich!) They returned with great tales about the world of tomorrow and showed me a picture of an exhibit of a city of the future. It depicted high speed commuter trains, spaceships, and tall buildings. Religion was not forgotten in this model of the city of tomorrow. I noticed on a quiet hillside, outside the limits of the city and far removed from the center of activity, an old-fashioned church building with a steeple and the other traditional trappings of church architecture. The secondary role assigned to religion among the secular wonders of this futuristic city, as conceived by an artist forty years ago, reflects an evaluation of religion that is too prevalent.

One of the dilemmas troubling religious people of every age is just how involved to become with secular things. The founder of the Christian faith once observed that his followers were to be "in" the world but not "of" the world. Religious writers of varying faiths may differ on points of doctrine, but usually agree that "the faithful" court danger if they allow themselves to be tainted by the secular world.

It is not surprising that people reared in a deeply religious atmosphere are extremely cautious about engaging in secular pursuits such as politics. Some suggest that the goals of the major religious faiths of America and the goals of politics in America are so contrary that each must be the mortal enemy of the other. Consequently, numerous Americans have decided to separate their religious feelings and their political convictions.

The consequence is apprehension whenever religion becomes an intricate part of a country's life. Fear arises that a civil religion may develop that shields us from religious experiences that are deep and abiding. And there is historical basis for these fears. Civil religion can cause us to believe we are experiencing the real thing when all we have in our grasp is a form of patriotism. Love of country and belief in the high ideals of the founding fathers are laudable but are no substitute for seeking and finding a religious faith by which to live out one's days.

I am not calling for a new form of civil religion. Nor am I suggesting the historical religious context within which mankind can best "find" its most meaningful relationship with God. What I am suggesting is that each person must look deep within and discover where the lines of his or her own faith are moored and to where they lead. Both the moorings and the ultimate destiny of a person's faith may be hazy, but in the act of seeking spiritual roots and destiny, a person can receive guidance for living life today. That person can understand that the vital connecting link between heritage and destiny is his or her own life. One may discover that the moral character ascribed to both heritage and destiny does, to an amazing degree, forecast the moral character of one's own life. A person's religious faith and way of life just cannot be separated.

Religion as a Way of Worship

The way people worship reveals what religion is about for them personally. What people worship with sincerity and without pretense provides clear evidence of what they believe.

To be born into a family with a long and deeply religious heritage can be either a curse or a blessing and is usually a little of both. Through the ages our ideas as to the origin and destiny of humankind have been in a constant state of change. It may seem from the vantage point of our own life that religious ideas are slow to change, but from a historical perspective, the religious ideas of humanity are a colorful kaleidoscope. They are in different forms and reveal a variety of personalities. However, there is a common strain running through them all. Central to all is the quest for an understanding of whatever power there be beyond us and before we ever existed. A religious faith that provides even partial satisfaction to the thirst for knowledge of the eternal is helpful in leading us to a deeper appreciation of our daily existence.

My own religious heritage, the faith of my fathers, is the Christian faith, which evolved from the Jewish religion. The Judeo-Christian faith holds much in common with many of the world's other major religions. Although the ways of worship differ from religion to religion, each worship form seeks to express the convictions of its adherents.

Sometimes I find persons resentful of the faith of their fathers. They feel they have outgrown the need their ancestors had for various forms of worship experiences. This resentment frequently results in their withdrawing from participation in the worship and institutional life of their historical faith.

Often, as persons mature, they find new meanings in the worship practices of their forebears. Although they may not be able to accept the literal meanings attached by their ancestors to their worship practices, they do recognize that there was a reality with which their ancestors were trying to relate in the faith. If people's faith provides them with "spiritual renewal," let there be rejoicing that a way of worship has been discovered that reminds them what their religion is about.

The religious faith of persons expressed through their ways of living and through their ways of worship is held in trust for future generations. But while they hold that faith and while it motivates their lives and stirs their religious devotion, they must avail themselves of its fruits that the nourishment might be theirs.

What many cold and intellectually isolated thinkers do not recognize is that, "unlike the great pyramids," as John Gardner points out, ". . . the monuments of the spirit will not stand untended. They must be nourished in each generation by the allegiance of believing men and women." [10] When people no longer care what happens in society, there can be no progress. Great civilizations are destroyed by apathy and lowered motivations, just as they are built by persons with sensitive hearts and strong spirits.

The heart . . . the spirit: these are terms that call forth feelings, and for most persons, religion becomes real only when the heart is touched and the spirit is stirred. Whenever society is confronted with persons living out their deepest faith in the midst of everyday life, something spiritually dynamic and emotionally moving is happening.

What it all comes down to is this: What a person personally believes is what motivates his actions; few persons can be detached and unemotional about what they do day in and day out. Out of spiritual introspection emerges a person's form of religion, molded by family, religious, and cultural heritage. Unless one is very unusual (and unfortunate), a person will feel deeply about this religion that she or he isolates and owns.

I am of the firm conviction that this nation needs citizens who deeply believe in the availability of the power of God to bring about changes that ought to be made in this country. The need, put in theological terminology, is for persons who are willing to wait for God because they believe he does respond to those who call upon him for help.

Religious institutions can help individuals deepen their faith in God. They can inspire a mutual reliance on him who is, "from everlasting to everlasting our God." They can remind us that the ways of human beings are transient—as a watch in the night, but that the ways of God are eternal and last forever.

The United States faces a critical need for persons and families and religious groups who are determined to wait for the Lord. Too many have gone off on their own and have waited for power, prestige, money, fame, fortune or whatever might bring them sensual joy. The great contribution of the world's living religions, through the centuries, has been in reminding not only their adherents, but the whole world that there is a God who made us all, from whom we came, and upon whom the wise wait. What modern people need more than anything else is to experience the presence of God in all areas of life—religious, political, social.

When one steps back and takes a long look at life today in its totality in this nation and, when in scanning the horizon of American life, its moral and ethical contours are seen clearly, it is pathetically apparent that refusal to wait upon God for his answers to the problems of life is causing havoc in area after area.

In the light of the disturbing national trends, and in view of the obvious refusal of so many to wait upon God for his divine guidance, what can be done to eradicate spiritual lethargy? Can "they that wait upon the Lord"—those who believe in God and support his religious institutions with their time and money—make a positive contribution toward reversing these tragic trends that are so evident?

I believe the answer is a simple but firm "yes." I think dedicated persons can contribute positively and powerfully to setting a spiritual tone for this generation by setting a spiritual tone for their own individual lives. National trends revealing the departure of persons from obedience to the ways of God are the collective representation of the exit of countless individuals from the household of faith.

Too many Americans are wallowing in ethical sloth, moral gluttony, and materialistic intemperance. Multitudes in this nation are on a secularistic binge, secure in the feeling that God will deliver them from any unfortunate consequences of their own spiritual poverty. They do little to deepen their personal relationship with God and sometimes even belittle those who dare suggest there is a desperate need in this nation for more persons who wait upon the Lord.

If there is even a measure of truth in what I am contending, it follows that more persons must become willing to devote a greater amount of their time and energy to strengthening their own personal relationship with God. There must arise a multitude of fathers and mothers and their offspring who insist that the sovereignty of the ways of God never be questioned in the conduct of family life. And, most important, there must be a renewal of substantial support for the religious institutions which are the ultimate custodians, that stump that remains after the forest is all but destroyed.

With conviction and feeling, each of us must face up to what religion is all about for us personally. Only after we have extracted from our thoughts and feelings the religious beliefs that are the motivating force behind our actions are we prepared to consider how religion and politics can or should be mixed in our lives.

What Politics Is About

The American political scientist, Robert Stahl, once defined politics as "who gets what, when, where and how." Aristotle maintained that "man is by nature a political animal!"

When people get together they inevitably want the same things and thus the potential for conflict is born. The process of politics will determine who gets what. Those decisions will not be made in a moral vacuum. "Politics will," as Reinhold Niebuhr claims, "to the end of history, be an area where conscience and power meet, where the ethical and coercive factors of human life will interpenetrate and work out their tentative and uneasy compromises."[12]

If politics consists of deciding matters that affect groupings of persons, and if within those groups individuals feel deeply about matters in ways far different from others in the same group, the potential for conflict is apparent. Even though agreement may be reached by all sides giving in a little on what they deeply believe, the "uneasy compromise" of which Niebuhr speaks may indeed be tentative. This is because, as Niebuhr himself observes, "individuals have a moral code which makes the actions of collective man an outrage to their conscience."[13] As a consequence, romantic and moral interpretations of real facts obscure rather than reveal the true character of human collective behavior. This results in what Niebuhr describes as "one of the real tragedies of the human spirit: its inability to conform its collective life to its individual ideals."

Religion is so intensely personal that its social and political application is extremely complicated. The relevance of individual religious ideals to collective situations does not involve a simple enlargement of the ideals to include many persons instead of one. Immediately there may surface contradictory ideals nurtured by the individual religious convictions of members of the group. The search for a common, collective religious ideal may require a flexibility difficult for some persons to accept.

It is not surprising that politics does not appear to be a realm in which persons of deep religious conscience can function effectively. How can persons who believe in specific religious principles compete in a game whose rules require compromise?

The answer is twofold.

First, there is no alternative if the religiously sensitive person is concerned about the welfare of all persons who live together in groups. There are rules that govern how persons live within these various groupings. If religious people fail to assist in working out those rules, there is almost no chance that the framework of government will reflect the values of sacred beliefs.

Second, the power of that goodness which religious persons attempt to bring to political decision-making must not be underestimated. If governmental entities are to establish policies that do provide for the welfare of the whole, the inclusion of moral values held by persons of religious persuasion is essential.

There will be, and should be, the expression of other values. Some of these values will complement religiously rooted values and some will be in contradiction to them. But there is no way religiously rooted values can be considered in the decision-making process until they are presented. Sometimes the secularists will advance values common to religion, but it is dangerous and irresponsible to depend on secularists to perform this function. If religious values are to be considered in collective decision-making, persons of religious faith must do whatever is necessary to assure their consideration.

The newpaper columnist Carl T. Rowan advanced an argument with which most religiously sensitive citizen-politicians agree when he wrote that "we can never bind this nation's wounds—physical, social or psychological—until we find leadership that is imbued with a special gift of applying goodness and compassion to the execution of public policy."[14] Persons of religious faith must equip themselves to provide this leadership.

Public policy decisions that disregard moral and ethical values common to the great religions of history carry within themselves the seeds of their own destruction. Morality is not an option to be refused, either on a personal or social level, without disastrous consequences. Call it nature, or the divine order of things, or something else, the reality most persons call God is there, and through the centuries men and nations have suffered because they disregarded God's claim to their allegiance.

The intricacies of political involvement will be discussed in later chapters. For the moment, I want to emphasize the need for persons to devote the time necessary to understand how the political process works. This is required of religiously sensitive citizen-politicians because of their conviction that goodness is relevant to the collective life of all. They thus come to the rational conclusion that they must get involved in politics. Otherwise, they are abetting the deprivation of the ethical influence of religion from a vast area of life where critical decisions are made.

But the true scope of religion and politics cannot be realized until religiously sensitive citizen-politicians understand the limitations of both.

The comedian Red Skelton was once heard to say: "You ought not get too upset about life because you're not going to get out of it alive anyhow!" Skelton would probably agree that persons do not have it within their power to solve the vast ethical and moral problems which dot the political landscape.

John Gardner, who has devoted a sizable portion of his life trying to imbue the political processes of America with a higher degree of ethical sensitivity, still has the good judgment to observe that "the man who dedicates his life to the achieving of good government or to the combating of human misery may enjoy small victories, but he can never win the longer battle."[15] The heartaches and trials of this world can never be escaped as long as there is life, regardless of how politically active and spiritually sensitive we may become.

On the national political scene in America one of the most persistent advocates of mixing religion and politics has been Oregon's United States Senator Mark Hatfield. He has written books, made numerous speeches on and off the floor of the Senate, introduced legislation, amended bills, and in other ways witnessed to his belief that religious values are worthy of being guidelines for America's political process. Hatfield says his reason for personal involvement in the fields of politics and religion is "not with the expectation that we will produce the Kingdom of God, but rather that we will be obedient to the imperatives of God and witness to his Spirit's working in our individual and corporate life."[16]

My goal is to encourage a new excellence in the practice of mixing religion and politics. To achieve such excellence requires discipline and tenacity. To hold such aspirations requires the discipline to search diligently within oneself for a clear understanding of what one believes. One must ask the hard question: Of what importance are my beliefs to the political decisions affecting lives so dramatically? A person must be willing to give time and mental energy to learn what politics is about, how it works, and how to become effective in the political realm. Above all else, a person must have the grit to keep at the task after repeated failures and in spite of the opinions of others that all efforts are in vain.

Religiously sensitive persons who develop such a philosophy are making a mature acceptance of their responsibility as human beings. This responsibility they accept, not to save the world, for they know they can no more save the world than their forefathers could. Rather, they accept the responsibility of mixing religion and politics to save themselves from the terrible fate of meaninglessness which awaits those who refuse to come to terms with their faith, the world in which they live, and the God who made them.

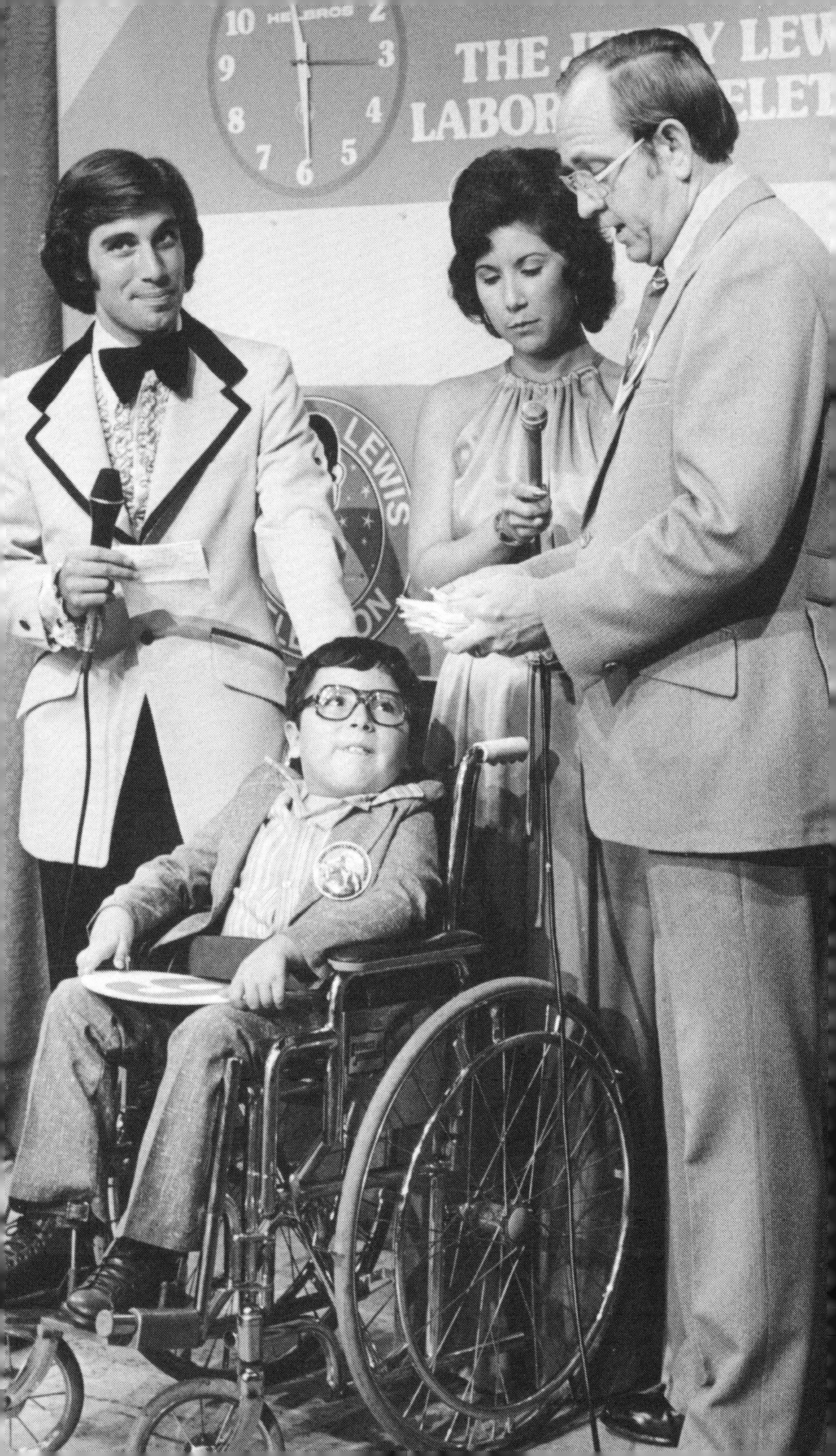

3

The Many Faces of Religiously Sensitive Politicians

Religiously sensitive politicians are not a group! The varieties of opinion among them are frequently greater than the differences between some of them and avowed secularists. Depth of conviction is characteristic of most religiously sensitive persons and deeply held convictions can lead to alienation from those holding contrary beliefs.

A prime reason for apprehension about religiously sensitive politicians in the political world is that they seem to speak in contradictory words; they appear with many faces. The four faces discussed in this chapter are among those most frequently seen.

Religiously sensitive persons become involved in politics because of what they believe, and they express those convictions through what they do. The actions of the first three types of citizen-politicians are distinguished mainly by what they believe. The activity of the fourth group is distinguished mainly by its preoccupation with one form of political action. The faces of purists, separatists, and accommodators convey a deeply felt urgency for political decision-makers to heed what they believe. Resolutionists are those who attach great significance to passing of resolutions as a primary means of influencing the political process.

Religiously sensitive citizen-politicians are not always consistent and frequently move from one ideological position to another, depending on the political issue under consideration. They may follow one procedure in dealing with a specific issue and adopt another procedure to confront a different issue. Or they may switch ideological positions while being involved with a single issue.

A friend in the Missouri General Assembly once told me of a constituent who encouraged him to seek re-election. "We need you up there in the State Capitol to keep all those crooked politicians honest," the constituent said. He continued, "By the way, Senator, I've got a daughter taking the state examination for real estate salespersons next week. She's a good girl but has had a hard time finding a job. If she passes this exam, she has a job waiting for her. Do you reckon you could fix it so she'd be sure to pass that exam?"

This constituent was initially a purist as he began his conversation. He wanted to see the virtue of truth incorporated in the body politic. Before he finished he was an undesirable kind of accommodator. Such inconsistency, though usually not so obvious, damages the credibility of persons who claim to be interested in advancing political purity.

As we study the four faces, it should be apparent that absolute separation into pure groupings is neither advisable nor possible. The faces that religious persons present to the world can be seen readily, but what goes on in their minds is not always so visible.

The Purists

I have many friends who, in at least some respects, possess the characteristics of purists. But none are complete purists all the time and probably would be offended to be labeled purists. Ward level politics do not interest purists very much because purists tend to be preoccupied with issues and have little patience with the struggles for power among politicians and party factions that are the meat and bread of local politics.

Purists measure every situation by the ethical and moral standards they accept for their own lives. Material things, professional status, personal acclaim—these are of little concern in the personal world of most purists. But how things in this world actually are run, compared to how they ought to be run is a major concern that receives the undivided attention of purists.

Purists are solicitous about what they believe. They cannot bear to have their convictions tainted or stained by the ways of the world. They view compromise as the pollution of idealism. Purists seldom are comfortable with political compromises hammered out by legislative bodies. They are dissatisfied because politics never completely fulfill their ideals.

Purists are fine people. Those who truly fit the purist mold are not self-righteous, for they recognize human pride as the chief of our sins. But they are a thorn in the side of politicians. Their insistence on rigid adherence to ideals that are not identical with the collective aspirations of a politician's constituency make conflict between purists and politicians unavoidable. The confrontation of a politician, who feels loyalty to the collective views of the constituency, with a purist who feels loyalty to deeply held convictions, can be awesome. In a sense politicians become purists also, their immovable ideal being to defend and promote what they believe to be the wishes of their constituents.

It follows, then, that purists are often in conflict with other purists. Those who would dilute their ideals are foes to be converted, but those who take an opposite stand are enemies to be defeated. There are classic examples of adversary purists in American political life: pro-life versus free-choice abortion advocates, women's rights supporters versus foes of the Equal Rights Amendment, right-to-work proponents versus collective bargaining defenders, etc. In the politician's terminology, these purist groups represent "gut" issues that are extremely volatile. Many politicians try to avoid taking sides between adversary purists because they feel the result is always a "no-win" situation in campaigning for election to public office.

Purists are convinced there are right and proper ways for people to be governed that can be readily ascertained. They take a position very similar to the natural law theory of the patron saint of Roman Catholicism, St. Thomas Aquinas.

St. Thomas, who lived in the thirteenth century, based his teachings concerning natural law on earlier views of the classical Greek philosopher, Aristotle. "Natural" was defined by Aristotle as that which has the same force everywhere and does not exist merely by people's thinking this or that. St. Thomas defines nature as a reason put into things by the divine art so that they move to a determinate end. These two thinkers insisted that things happen because their very nature requires it. The source of their nature is God who is not unconcerned about what people do. St. Thomas claims that: "In order, therefore, that man may know without any doubt what he ought to do and what he ought to avoid, it was necessary for man to be directed in his proper acts by a law given by God, for it is certain that such a law cannot err."[17]

People can, and do, disagree in their interpretation as to what that natural law is. Who is going to decide among conflicting claims? According to Professor Charles N. R. McCoy of the Catholic University of America, St. Thomas believed "the Church, [i.e., the Roman Catholic Church] as the guardian of the divine law, claims the right to decide"[18] what is by nature of God.

It is at this point that Protestants, Jews, and adherents of other religious faiths part company with Roman Catholics. They refuse to assign the Roman Catholic Church the role as the divinely selected proclaimer of the natural law for all persons for all time.

But it is not only the Roman Catholic Church that claims this prerogative. Other religious institutions and personages often assume this role for themselves without recognizing that they are doing so. And in a sense, each person, moment by moment, deciding what he ought to do, is responding to the necessity to make a judgment as to what nature compels him to do.

The purists are convinced that the positions they take are right; they are what ought to be; they are the natural choices a prudent person would make. Consequently, they cannot understand when views contrary to their own are advanced.

Thomas Jefferson wrote, "The whole art of government consists in the art of being honest," implying that the honest position in every situation is obvious. Jimmy Carter, before he became President, wrote that the leadership America should provide the rest of the world "need not depend on our inherent military force, or economic power, or political persuasion. It should derive from the fact that we try to be right and honest and truthful and decent."[19]

As Shakespeare would put it, "Ah, there's the rub." How do we gain agreement on what is right, honest, truthful, and decent? Take a vote? Let a religious body decide? Consult the stars? Turn it over to the academic community for decision? Take a public opinion poll and find out what the people think?

The purist says, "Listen to me." And he or she may be right, or that person may be wrong. But the purist does have a position and possesses the courage to express it. Most religiously sensitive persons start out as purists. They get involved in politics because they believe in certain principles and are convinced their ideals ought to be incorporated in the laws that govern how people shall live together.

James Q. Wilson, a Harvard professor, did a masterful study of newcomers—amateurs—in politics. He concluded that amateurs insist politicians ought to work for certain ends purely because they are convinced of the intrinsic worth of those ends. He noted that "the amateur, unlike the professional, must feel that any rewards other than the satisfaction of serving a good cause and idealized principles are and must be secondary. . . ."[20]

As the amateurs participate in politics, they are certain to be confronted with many challenges to their purist positions. Then comes the soul-searching and intellectual questioning as to the validity of their views. If they come out of this internal struggle with their position intact, they may renew their efforts to penetrate policy with their views, or they may consider their ideals impossible to attain in the public realm and retreat from political involvement in apathy and discouragement.

The way of the purist in an imperfect world is not easy. If Reinhold Niebuhr is correct that "religion is always a citadel of hope . . . built on the edge of despair," the purist requires a religious faith to keep spirits high and ideals resolute. The religiously oriented purists do not expect the fulfillment of their ideals in their lifetimes. They can do what they feel is necessary and leave the rest to the determination of eternity. Many hardened professionals in the political world call such resignation foolishness. To others it has a wistful appeal that makes the purist, even in the moment of failure, a personality admired but unheeded; respected but lonely.

The Separatists

The separatists in American political life are persons who accept as both their religious and political mission the maintenance of a wall of separation between church and state.

Thomas Jefferson, in a letter to a committee of the Danbury, Connecticut, Baptist Association, originated the concept of "a wall of separation between Church and State." Jefferson felt the restriction on Congress in the First Amendment to "make no law respecting an establishment of religion, or prohibiting the free exercise thereof"[21] effectively removed government from any involvement with religious institutions.

Actually the origin of the separation of religious concerns from governmental administration occurred long before Jefferson's time. Professor George H. Sabine writes, "The rise of the Christian church, as a distinct institution entitled to govern the spiritual concerns of mankind in independence of the state, may not unreasonably be described as the most revolutionary event in the history of western Europe, in respect both to politics and political philosophy."[22]

Previous to this separation, after the Roman Emperor Constantine became a Christian in A.D. 325 and declared his domain to be the Holy Roman Empire, the influence of the Roman Catholic Church in temporal and governmental affairs was extensive. Centuries before in the Hebrew nation, the religious and governmental institutions were intertwined. Throughout history the relationship between governing entities and religious institutions of states and nations generally has been one of close cooperation if not identical organizational structure.

The roots of separatism in America are more secular than they are religious. This fact is alluded to by one of our nation's vocal separatists, Paul Blanshard. I recall reading in a book by Blanshard that more than 90 percent of the American people were outside all churches when the nation was founded. The presence of so many non-church people was probably a basic cause of the early emphasis in American history on preserving both religious freedom and the separation of church and state. In fact, most of the early colonists who were members of churches were quite intolerant and did not guarantee religious freedom or political rights.

The churches in colonial days, not unlike religious institutions of any culture, were purist organizations. They believed their position on how persons should live together to be divinely given; they had little patience with any who disagreed. Blanshard is probably correct that the secularist bent of America's early population contributed decisively to the traditional American insistence that the institutions and authority of religion and government be kept separate.

Another writer on church-state relations, Thomas Sanders, insists that the separatist view has become so ingrained in American thought that "Americans, especially laymen, take democracy and separation of church and state to be political arrangements specially favored by God."[23] The separatists are not receptive to suggestions that there are constitutionally valid, politically possible, and religiously appropriate ways for religion to interact with government. Their mission is, at all costs, to keep not only institutionalized religion but any organized or structured expression of religion from entanglement with government at any level.

The methods of the separatists are frequently militant, usually narrowly focused, moderately pragmatic, and generally the expression of devout and sincere convictions rooted in a fear that both religion and government will suffer if permitted too close an association.

The separatists make frequent use of political power to preserve the practice of separatism in American government. Their most consistent opposition is to efforts to secure funds for educational institutions maintaining any connection with a religious body. Candidates for public office are opposed, and not infrequently defeated, on the basis of their stand on some aspect of separatism.

Separatists, like many other religiously sensitive persons, are not always consistent. When I decided to run for public office and retain my standing as an active clergymen, I was reprimanded by the executive secretary of the Missouri Council of Churches who insisted that I should have resigned my pastorate the day I announced for public office because I was contributing to an excessive entanglement of church and state. After I was elected, he reprimanded me again because my vote on a certain issue did not reflect what he considered to be the view of the church. "After all," he said, "being a clergyman in the legislature, you are supposed to represent the views of the church." I reminded him I did not seek office to represent the views of the church but of the 28,000 people who lived in my district. I told him I hoped my religious convictions had a positive influence on my political views but that in no sense was I an official representative of the church. In my opinion, the position he was taking was in direct contradiction to his separatist stance.

Separatists are found in many religious groups but are most numerous among Baptists and Jews. Organizationally they are represented by Protestants and Other Americans United for Separation of Church and State, which was formed in 1948. Separatists have been active in state legislatures and in Congress and have participated in financing lawsuits seeking to gain court decisions favorable to their position.

Sometimes separatists are mistakenly thought to advocate keeping political life free of the high moral and ethical principles common to most religions. Admittedly their actions may have this effect but such a result is not the intention of the separatists of my acquaintance. These misunderstandings persist because compromise is foreign to the separatist's mode of operation. Separatists are so convinced of the critical need for an absolute separation of church and state that they may refuse to support a public policy commendable in other respects if they feel it fails to maintain the proper relationship between ecclesiastical and political institutions. Separatists are devout persons who are convinced that they must mix religion and politics on their own terms if the virtues of separation of church and state in America are to be preserved.

The Accommodators

The dictionary defines an accommodator simply as "a person or thing that accommodates."

I considered other titles as possibilities, especially that of compromiser. Compromise is a necessary ingredient in politics, and plays a role in the interfacing of religion and politics.

In order to understand the role of the accommodator, a cursory consideration of the role of the compromiser is advisable. Essential to the success of the compromiser is a willingness for two sides in a dispute to yield—to meet halfway (or nearly so) between their respective positions. Neither side is wholly comfortable with the compromise position because each realizes the degree of variance from their original position. However, since compromisers have to work out an agreement, they may endure tampering with what they feel to be true if it can gain them even a temporary settlement.

In contrast, the purpose of the accommodator is to bring into harmony or agreement one person or position with another person or position, with each retaining its basic nature. The accommodator tries to make it possible for religious principles and the political process to be in harmony without either having to violate their intended purposes. This cannot be done if one does not look truth in its face, whether that truth be grounded in religion or politics. What is false cannot be made truth and what is truth cannot be made false.

The accommodator's task is to satisfy the need of the political process for religious guidance. Truth, which is the bulwark of religion can and will be interpreted in varying ways, but it cannot be willfully compromised. A religious purist attempting to bear witness to the principle of the God whom he seeks to serve, does not bear the face of a compromiser. Any person who is in politics to barter away the principles of faith will be miserable. The compromises may bring temporary relief in a difficult situation, but provide no lasting solution to the critical need in politics for the truth found in religion.

Accommodators resist the temptation to permit uneasy accommodation between religious principles and political expediency. They know that religion and politics can never be mixed on any other basis than through the maintenance of the essential integrity of each.

Persons who appear as accommodators provide the best picture of religiously sensitive citizen-politicians. Accommodators are aware that the opinions of the political world and those of the religious world, as to what rules ought to guide our behavior, are frequently far apart. Their purpose is to bring into agreement or harmony the ways and goals of politics and the ways and goals of religion. Accommodators are advocates of peace among conflicting forces. Being in the middle, they are battered from both sides and never really feel at home in either camp.

Philosophically and practically, the title of Reinhold Niebuhr's famous book, *Moral Man and Immoral Society,* describes the situation in which accommodators usually find themselves. But they must beware lest they think they have achieved moral perfection. The illusion of such grandeur can make them unfit to fulfill their accommodating role between politics and religion.

True accommodators are too familiar with the imperfection of humanity to believe they are exceptions to the general tendency of us all to think more highly of ourselves than the facts justify. If accommodators get to believing that their opinions are identical with those of God, they cease to be effective.

The object of accommodators is not to accommodate themselves, but their religious principles to the world of politics. If they find themselves trying to put square pegs in round holes, they know they must search until they find some round pegs or square holes. Accommodators cultivate the art of the possible and refuse to waste time in a futile quest for the unattainable.

To illustrate, in most parts of the world it is recognized that the body requires some sort of cushion to lie on if it is to be refreshed by periods of rest and sleep. Some use straw, others coiled springs enclosed in cotton, others foam rubber, and still others a cushion of water. The principle: the body needs a comfortable place to rest. The method: use whatever materials are available and whatever custom dictates to accommodate the need of the body for rest.

The accommodator has the task of convincing religious persons and groups that their basic principles are identical with those of politicians and the governments they serve. Obviously the methods developed in the two worlds will vary because the immediate tasks require a variety of procedures. The ultimate goal, though, of governments and religions is the same—to assure every person the opportunity to become the best person possible. Religions are convinced that a major factor in achieving this goal is a person's response to God. Religious bodies therefore expend considerable effort through education and worship to make persons aware of God and his desires for humanity.

Governments are convinced that persons cannot achieve their potential without economic, physical, mental, and social security. Government institutions are created to assure such security, and laws are enacted to permit private enterprise to assume responsibility for providing such security.

It is inevitable that two powerful forces in society which embark on the same course will come face to face on many occasions. There is no reason why they cannot accommodate each other without compromising major principles. They are not enemies pursuing different objectives but potential friends seeking the accomplishment of common goals. Because their functions are different, they may have contrasting organizational patterns and sources of authority. But often the very nature of their labors throws them into each other's company. The good of persons is served best when they walk together as friends. Accommodators accept the challenge to do what they can to make religion and politics as compatible as reason and circumstances dictate.

Among those who actually share the aspirations of accommodators but believe successful accommodation impossible is a group we could call "the haters." I recall writing an article at a year's end noting the fiscal impact of state government's expenditures on the economy of Missouri. An editorial appeared in one of the state's newspapers criticizing me for suggesting anything good could come out of evil government.

Admittedly government does not produce capital resources per se, but how it manages the resources put at its disposal has a great effect on its constituency. My detractor would probably admit this, but his more basic point is that government itself is evil. He and many other hostile citizens have come to hate government and see in its existence and growth the source of most, if not all, of society's problems.

People are frustrated by changing social mores, unstable economics, international challenges to America's assumed world leadership, and increased questioning by our young of moral values thought by most to be universally accepted. Government at any level, but especially big government as represented by the federal government and only to a slightly lesser degree by state government, is accused and found guilty by haters as both the cause and the consequence of these frustrations.

In a highly complex, interrelated, and increasingly technological world, frustration is likely to spread if orderly ways are not developed to handle the common problems of society. Human greed and imperfection being what they are, democratic government is necessary to ascertain the will of the majority of society and to institute rules of conduct that express that will, while preserving rights of the minority. Those who are wanting these rules to be based on ethical and moral principles of religion must cease the wasteful expenditure of mental effort and emotional outbursts that reflect their hatred of politics and government; they must become active accommodators.

The efforts of seven lay persons to be accommodators are discussed briefly in the next few pages. The first three are well-known public figures. The last four, two men and two women, have gained little fame outside their own communities. But all are united by the common conviction that religion and politics must be mixed. Each believes that if politics is to serve our needs it must receive the guidance, the leadership, and the inspiration of persons willing to apply their religious principles to their political participation.

An obvious accommodator is President Jimmy Carter. Opinions may vary as to the effectiveness of his political leadership, but few doubts are expressed about the depth and sincerity of his intention to accommodate religious principles and political procedures. Early in his administration he voiced strong support for an American foreign policy based on the concept of human rights for persons of every nation. His personal religious habits, such as regular worship attendance, and teaching a weekly church school class, provide outward evidence of the importance he attaches to the maintenance of his religious spirit. If President Jimmy Carter is not a deeply religious person—meaning one who believes in the presence and power of a Divine Being—he has a lot of people fooled.

In the fall of 1975, as a member of the Executive Committee of the Democratic Party of Missouri, I was frequently invited to attend small gatherings of party leaders to meet with candidates for the 1976 Democratic presidential nomination. Included was an invitation to join other party leaders for a private dinner in St. Louis with Jimmy Carter.

When I arrived at the dinner only three other party leaders were present, and one of them stayed for just a few minutes. The result was an hour and a half spent in stimulating discussion with a man who I felt, frankly, had little chance of becoming President. The predominant impressions Carter made on me were that he was sincere, slightly stubborn, supremely confident in himself, and devoutly religious. As President, his actions have confirmed my initial judgment. President Carter also is a sincere accommodator and has demonstrated that in the world's highest elected office, the accommodation of religion and politics is possible.

I would place near the top of the list of sincere and effective accommodators in public office two United States Senators—Harold Hughes, Democrat of Iowa, and Mark Hatfield, Republican of Oregon. Hughes decided to leave the Senate because he felt he could be more effective in witnessing to his faith away from the political mainstream. Hatfield was first elected to the Senate in 1966 after serving as Governor of Oregon and has continued to view public office as an appropriate realm in which to witness to his faith.

Harold Hughes' story is familiar. A reformed alcoholic and a former truck driver, he amazed the country with his election as Governor of Iowa. After election to the Senate, he emerged early as a leader to be heard. Among his major legislative interests were drug and alcoholic treatment programs and world peace. In 1972 he was mentioned frequently as a potential presidential candidate but withdrew his name from consideration. Shortly afterward he announced he would retire from the Senate at the end of his term to join a Christian businessmen's organization.

Hughes is credited by Charles Colson, legal adviser to President Richard Nixon at the time of the Watergate scandal, as being helpful during the early days after Colson's conversion to the Christian faith. The former Senator is a frequent speaker at governmental prayer breakfasts across the country. I am impressed with this huge man of rugged features who speaks so simply but powerfully of the need for reliance on God in the midst of America's political and governmental deliberations.

Senator Hatfield, a former college dean, brings conservative religious posture to his political activities which are frequently assessed as being traditionally liberal.

A message Hatfield delivered at Westminster College in Missouri in 1977, revealed his deep conviction that accommodators are critically needed to resolve today's political problems. He noted that "the problems we regard as political issues do involve basic spiritual dimensions and require of us a rigorous attempt to participate in God's equations for justice." Hatfield contended that "the erroneous proposition that religion and politics don't mix is breaking down," and went on to suggest: "We do not have to check our kingdom dreams and prophetic insights at the door of the arena of public discourse." He said to his audience: "Let us not abandon government as an 'unspiritual' realm. While institutions of church and state must remain separate, politics and morality must not be divorced. Greatly needed is a union of spiritual wisdom and political action."[24]

A pair of accommodators I know illustrate that accommodators may follow different paths to reach the same destination. These two men, both of whom lived in Marshall, Missouri, are about as different as any two men can be. One was a devout Protestant, a holder of public office for over forty years, an activist in his political party, and inclined to rely more on his personal powers of persuasion than organizational strength to accomplish his ends. The other man was an equally devout Roman Catholic. He served briefly as a city councilman but did not seek elective office again. Although a nominal member of a political party, he participated very little in its activities. He was extremely active in many community organizations. He was one of those persons willing to assume duties that others refused.

The first man, Frank McGraw, was presiding judge of Saline County. He possessed a faith profound in its simplicity that religious beliefs are applicable to service in public office. His concern for a good public school system, progressive welfare measures, adequate care for the aged poor, and honest, efficient administration of public funds were well known. Because Frank had run for office many times, he accumulated a flock of supporters and another group of people who always opposed him. The latter group was composed mainly of candidates whom he had defeated. This group was suspicious of his ethics and inclined to work against whatever he favored.

I found his religion to be real. The efforts of Judge McGraw to accommodate his public duties to his religious principles were tireless. For years I served as his pastor and have personal knowledge of many instances when he looked a controversy full in its face, asked of himself, "What is the morally right thing to do?" Then, without measuring the political consequences, Frank accommodated that political situation to his religious principles.

The second man, Leo Hayob, was a Roman Catholic in a predominantly Protestant community who attended mass at seven every morning. Nearly all of his fellow citizens, among whom he was almost universally recognized as the community's most effective leader-doer, knew he was Catholic but few were aware of the profound influence of religion in his life. If his fellow townspeople ever considered the depth and breadth of his involvement in nearly every worthwhile community endeavor, and knew that his economic gains from pushing these projects had been nil, they would have known there was a powerful source of motivation for this community dynamo.

I do not know all aspects of Leo's community involvement, but what I do know is impressive. It is difficult to envision one man successfully guiding so many different worthwhile projects, frequently at the same time. He was the driving force behind the conversion of a disreputable, dirty, and poorly run "County Poor Farm" into an efficiently operated and clean County Home for the Aged. An industrial development corporation that attracted many new industries to his community was founded under his auspices because he recognized the need for a broadly based local economy. As the part-time, underpaid executive of the Chamber of Commerce, he worked with both long and newly-established businesses and industries, assuring them of the appreciation of the community for the contribution made to its economic well-being.

Few meetings of the City Council were held without Leo Hayob's constructive but watchdog-like presence. He observed the presence of deteriorating areas in his town. After becoming familiar with federal and state programs of land clearance and housing, he accepted leadership of the Land Clearance Redevelopment Commission which cleansed the city of many rat-infested firetraps. Noting the poor housing of many of the community's low income residents, he led in the establishment of a local housing authority that erected three separate housing complexes. When a manager for these complexes could not be found, he took the job.

His accomplishments are endless: supporter of the local private college as a member and secretary of its Board of Trustees, moving force behind the raising of funds for the construction of a new county fairgrounds and leader in the movement to institute a

U. S. Senator Thomas F. Eagleton converses with Mr. Spainhower.

city-manager form of government. This man never allowed ideas to remain in the abstract. He got involved personally to guarantee that they became realities.

On many occasions, this outstanding accommodator shared with me in quiet moments the influence of religion in determining his public conduct. He believed he would be untrue to the teachings of his faith if he did not become involved in making his community a better place for all people. He was of the firm conviction that it takes united community action to resolve most public problems. It seemed natural for Leo Hayob to be the catalyst in accommodating the religious principle of the Golden Rule—" So whatever you wish that men would do to you, do so to them"—to collective efforts to solve public problems.

The two women accommodators I will describe, and the other male accommodator, are all activists. Every accommodator is an activist. The adaptation of religious principles to the political process cannot be accomplished by passive persons. Active participation in the public arena is always characteristic of accommodators. Persons who show the faces of accommodators to the world know they cannot expect the miraculous intervention of God to do what the eternal is depending on us to accomplish.

Acceptance of the mandate to participate actively in the resolution of public issues with moral and ethical ramifications is obvious in the lives of the Reverend and Mrs. Rhodes Thompson of St. Louis. Both are active in many church, community, and political endeavors that produce an effective mix of religious and political idealism.

Rhodes distributes leaflets for political candidates in whom he believes; circulates petitions for causes he advocates; gets involved in seeking community solutions for neighborhood problems; and through the years has been a rather prolific letter writer to political officeholders. In pulpit utterances he has been unafraid to speak out on controversial issues, but has also shown forebearance with those who hold differing views.

Lois accepts her family and local church responsibilities graciously and performs them well without complaint. An active member of her political party, she is often involved in the campaigns of individual candidates. She is disturbed by extensive problems confronting persons on welfare and is constantly trying to improve their plight. Lois makes personal contact with welfare agencies and with state legislators instrumental in determining welfare policies. She is a member of a group of persons who lobby the state legislature for changes in the law to provide better administrative procedures and more adequate appropriations for dependent children.

Both Rhodes and Lois make trips to the state capitol to do personal lobbying. Their religious faith teaches them that they are expected by God to help those in need. Without the constant prodding of accommodators like these two, the needs of the poor and the cause of justice would soon be overwhelmed in legislative bodies. Lobbyists for economic interests tend to disregard completely and sometimes actually oppose legislation designed to provide relief for those who cannot afford to employ lobbyists to protect their interests. The delicate points of justice, so instrumental in protecting basic human and civil rights, are frequently bypassed in the mad rush of economic interests to secure favored governmental treatment. The influence of such myopic lobbyists must be balanced and often checked by volunteer accommodators. Without their presence, government loses its soul and spirit.

Another accommodator is aggressive, bordering on being militant. Women's rights is her "bag," and she spares no efforts in advancing them. Mrs. Elaine Aber of Jefferson City, Missouri, is never reluctant to voice her opinions. The Equal Rights Amendment, the rights of minorities, the right of a woman to choose an abortion, and other "rights" occupy her time and labors. An active church member, she is persistent in trying to get her local congregation and its state and national organizations to be vocal in support of the causes in which she believes. A staunch member of her political party, she is untiring in her efforts to get it to champion her causes.

Every cause Elaine adopts has first undergone her close scrutiny to ascertain if it is, in her judgment, compatible with her religious faith. She must be satisfied that an accommodation logically can be made between her religious principles and a given cause before she begins her accommodating activities. Once she decides they are kindred souls, she is off to battle! Although many disagree with some of her stands, those who know her respect her and are convinced the stimulation provided by her active posture on issues attests to the fact that religion and politics do mix.

Through the dedicated efforts of accommodators these opportunities are being utilized and the result is, more often than not, a positive blending of religion and politics.

The Resolutionists

The last face of religiously sensitive citizen-politicans to be considered is that of resolutionists. These persons become involved in resolution-making as a consequence of substantive positions as a purist, a separatist, or an accommodator. Resolutionists are receiving special attention because so many well intentioned religiously sensitive citizen-politicians present to the political world the bland face of a resolutionist and nothing else.

Resolutionists conceive their task to be that of composing resolutions on issues. They become involved in getting them adopted by religious groups, sometimes reinforcing them with petitions, and forwarding the resolutions to public officials with the authority to decide the issue in question.

There are positive and negative consequences that flow from the labors of the resolutionists. Among the positive effects is the involvement of religious persons in an educational experience. Resolutions, for both the authors of the resolutions and those who must vote on them, encourage and permit a constructive consideration of important public issues. Resolutions well researched and thoroughly explained can even stimulate persons to do independent research. Such additional study may encourage these individuals to take a more responsible and informed position on issues.

My denomination, the Christian Church (Disciples of Christ), over a period of years has developed extensive but simple procedures for members and congregations to submit resolutions for the business docket of our biennial national meeting and for statewide meetings. Other religious groups have adopted similar procedures. These resolutions are printed and distributed several weeks before the meeting, thereby permitting the voting delegates to familiarize themselves with the resolutions and the issues they address.

The discussion of these resolutions during business sessions sometimes becomes quite heated. Those who carefully follow the deliberations learn a lot about many different subjects. It is an educational experience and some delegates, both before and after national or state meetings, involve their local congregations in a discussion of the issues. In this manner, the educational benefit is shared by thousands of persons who never actually participate in the final voting.

A second positive effect of the resolutionists is psychological. Persons become involved in actually trying to do something about a public problem. Instead of standing apathetically on the sidelines, persons are encouraged to consider what they, personally, think about an issue.

A third effect, which is the end purpose of a resolutionist's activity, is the possibility of prodding a legislative body, a branch of governmental bureaucracy, or some other public entity into action. The positions religious groups take on public issues can sometimes affect the determination of public policy.

On the negative side of the ledger, the first defect in the work of many resolutionists is that they are inadequately informed and base their position on false information. Too often a religious body knows what position it wants to take and proceeds to formulate a resolution that will support that position. In their passion for their cause, they fail to present the issue fairly. When their resolution is received by those familiar with the total situation, its presentation of only part of the total picture weakens not only the effectiveness of the resolution but also the credibility of the group submitting the resolution.

A second negative aspect of some resolutionists is their naive assumption that they actually are conveying the sentiments of most of the members of their group. What is worse, they may know their resolutions do not represent the actual sentiments of their group but still persist in their resolution activity. They may not even admit to themselves, let alone in public, that they are not authorized to speak for their membership. In some cases they may state that they do not speak for their religious bodies but then proceed as if their actions do represent the feelings of their group.

The consequences can be quite damaging. Resolutions from certain, if not all religious bodies, are of questionable effectiveness because public officials doubt how accurately they reflect their group's collective opinion. Few groups, especially American religious bodies, are so monolithic in either composition or thought as to hold to one opinion with much consistency. The plurality of American life increasingly is evident in the membership of major religious bodies. While a religious group may develop some consistency with respect to its opinions on public issues, in recent years the ability of even such traditionally monolithic groups as the Roman Catholics and the Southern Baptists to hold their members together on public issues has greatly diminished. Not all Roman Catholics are opposed to birth control and not all Southern Baptists oppose the provision of public bus transportation for all school children. Public awareness of the divergent thinking within religious bodies has made it more and more difficult for a religious body to be effective in the public arena through the labors of their resolutionists.

A third negative for resolutionists is the tendency for their efforts to be divisive within the groups they represent. In one of the national meetings of my denomination a position of "let's study the matter further" was adopted in regard to legal rights for homosexuals. One member, in a letter to the editor of the denomination's magazine, voiced an opinion frequently expressed. "We need to be challenged to think and act on such issues as . . . homosexuality. . . . But to count a vote on such issues . . . is a practice so divisive that we can no longer afford it." Another reader confessed he "was bothered, as were a great number of others, by the tension in the debates over the controversial issues. . . ."

Any group, religious or otherwise, needs wise leadership imbued with the ability to judge how much divisive argument can be endured without impairing the group's capacity to act unitedly and effectively.

A final negative result, and perhaps the most unfortunate, is that the effort of the resolutionist may be very successful on the surface. The religious body passes the resolution with enthusiasm. News of their action is promptly conveyed to the proper authorities. The members of the group return home and dismiss the matter from their minds. To their way of thinking, they met the issue on the convention floor, dealt with it and now proceed to other matters.

Resolutionists do not generally solve any problems. They talk about problems and may even suggest solutions, but the action always remains to be taken. The problem with most religious persons, especially clergymen, is that they are so accustomed to talking about issues, they subconsciously conclude that to speak about an issue is all that is necessary.

Lyndon Johnson once observed that "It is the politician's task to pass legislation, not sit around saying principled things."[25] Religious people are fond of mouthing principles. Their approval of a resolution that speaks in eloquent words of slaying public dragons makes their blood run hot. Once the resolution-passing gathering is adjourned, the excitement of the moment subsides, and the participants return to their usual daily activities, convinced they have done their religious duty.

How mistaken they are. The critical mixing opportunities for the religiously sensitive are not to be found in the activities of resolutionists. Mixing religion and politics as it ought to be done is not so simple as passing a resolution. As a minimum effort, participation in the political party of one's choice is advisable.

4

The Party Isn't Over!

When David Broder's book about American political parties was published in the early seventies with the title *The Party's Over*, many assumed this noted political columnist was announcing the demise of the political party as a viable mechanism for politics in this country. Actually, Broder was attracting the reading public's attention by using a catchy phrase to express a growing sentiment among Americans that political parties have outlived their usefulness. Public faith in political parties ranges from weak to almost nonexistent. The Party is over for many Americans. They want no part of being identified as a member of any political party.

Persons with religious concerns are not much different from the rest of the population in this regard. There is widespread apprehension of political party involvement among religiously oriented persons. Even persons considered by their religiously active peers to be politically active are usually conspicuous by their absence from political party activity.

The opinion is frequently expressed that although religious persons are obligated to witness to religious principles in the world of politics and government, they must be cautious in identifying with a particular political party. It is assumed political party participation contaminates, tarnishes, and hampers efforts to translate lofty religious ideas into public policy.

My contention is that the prevailing reluctance of religiously sensitive persons to participate in political parties is ill-advised, borders on naivete, and contributes to the ineffectiveness of many conscientious religious persons in influencing critical public decisions. If religious truths are to influence public policy decisions of government, the party isn't over for the religiously sensitive citizen-politician.

Broder insists government must be served by strong political parties if it is to meet its responsibilities. He contends that America has suffered governmental stalemate because the nation has not used the political party as an instrument to discipline government to meet its needs. His book's title is misleading—intentionally. His thesis, that the American attitude toward political parties has been irresponsible, is sound. If political parties are permitted to wither, the resultant damage to the legitimate work of government will be extensive.

It is time for persons who recognize the need to mix religion and politics to get rid of the illusion that they can be effective at this task and continue to disregard political parties. The party is not over as a viable instrument for fashioning governmental policies. Nor is the party over as an appropriate channel through which to funnel the ideals of religion.

Religiously sensitive citizen-politicians bear a personal responsibility to assist in restoring political parties to positions of public esteem and leadership. For persons like Broder, whose aim is to help government to be more responsible, and for persons whose aim is to help government be expressive of the highest values, strong political parties are a necessity. This insistence on the fundamental role of political parties does not enjoy universal acceptance, especially among religiously sensitive persons. Many Americans continue to ask, "Why do we need political parties?"

Why We Have Political Parties

Just because an organization exists is not, in itself, sufficient justification to continue its existence. But if the reasons for its existence are understood, judgment usually can be made as to whether the organization should be continued.

Political parties have not always been a feature on the American political landscape. Our founding fathers were suspicious of factions and parties. They believed the causes which led them to rebel against the British were sufficiently unifying to compel Americans to be of one mind. Consequently when they wrote the Constitution, they made no provision for political parties. The American political party movement was not intended by Washington or other early leaders such as Jefferson and Madison.

In fashioning a system for the election of a President, Madison and others at the Constitutional Convention did not allow for political factionalism. They planned the election of a President to be an intellectual exercise among the nation's brightest and best leaders. The name given to the organization devised to elect the nation's President, "The Electoral College," reveals how firmly they believed that the choosing of a President should be an intellectual process. Their method was this: Bring together the brightest and best men (and they literally meant men, no women) from each of the states, put them in a room, let them debate the merits of the various candidates, and the best man would be chosen.

Their system worked well as long as George Washington was willing to serve. He was held in such high esteem that nearly everyone agreed he ought to be President. Even Jefferson, who felt uneasy over the perpetual eligibility of a President, said he did not want the situation changed "as long as we can avail ourselves of the services of our great leader, whose talents and whose weight of character, I consider as peculiarly necessary to get the government so under way, as that it may afterwards be carried on by subordinate characters . . ." [26] But when Washington let it be known during his second term that he would not serve another, factionalism, partisanship, and policy disagreements began to emerge. Gradually sentiments solidified behind two men, John Adams the Vice President and Thomas Jefferson the Secretary of State. Followers of each felt their man best equipped to succeed Washington and in the efforts to support these two candidates are found the organizational beginnings of American political parties. Followers of Adams supported a strong national government and were known as Federalists. Jefferson's followers believed in more decentralization, or greater power residing in the states, and were called Republicans.

In the years since, the political party movement has continued. Alignments and interests have vacillated between two major parties. In America significant political party strength is rarely enjoyed outside the two major parties. Today's Republican party lies mainly in the tradition of the early Federalists, and the modern day Democratic party traces its lineage to Jefferson and the views of those who were then called Republicans, although emphases and directions have changed through the years.

Thomas Jefferson affords an interesting study of a man who personally distrusted and discouraged the formation of political parties and yet unwittingly founded one. While in Paris in 1789 he wrote to a friend in America: "I never submitted the whole system of my opinions to the creed of any party of men whatever, in religion, in philosophy, in politics or in anything else, where I was capable of thinking for myself." He emphasized how deeply he felt about the subject of parties by claiming that "if I could not go to heaven but with a party, I would not go there at all." [27]

American political parties are not, and really never have been, ideologically oriented. The object of the parties has been to put together a group that can win on election day and govern effectively afterwards. Doris Kearns, one of President Lyndon Johnson's biographers, writes that Johnson was vigorous in his insistence that American political parties "offering the nation a clear cut choice between fundamental principles would result in a nation grinding to a halt, consumed by irreconcilable argument, powerless to produce anything for anyone. He was convinced that an insistence on 'principled platforms' would wreck the two-party system by making impossible an alliance between men of disparate convictions, and encourage the emergence of many single-issue parties." [28] Johnson advocated loose parties and unifying leaders. He argued that a party representing only one group or one section could produce a consistent program, but that it was difficult to keep such parties alive.

Political parties are needed in a democracy to be the focal point through which the will of the majority is brought to bear on problems which affect every citizen but which must be addressed by a government strong enough to solve them. The political party which consistently lacks the muscle to win elections will never have the opportunity to use what muscle it does have to solve society's common problems.

The power to govern is so critical to a political party that it frequently becomes the only motivation for some party members. The professional politician, even the "professional" who practices politics as a hobby rather than as a vocation, is preoccupied with winning. Every other concern is a distant second for most politicians.

This emphasis on winning turns off some religiously sensitive citizen-politicians. Victory at any cost is not their idea of an appropriate strategy for mixing religion and politics. But if they are to learn how to function effectively in the political world, they have to understand, and actually have empathy for, the emphasis placed on winning by political parties.

Ultimately, of course, an enlightened political party strategy recognizes that for a party to pursue victory without regard for its basic purposes will be self-destructive. Lyndon Johnson, one of the most able politicians ever to occupy the presidency, once observed that "The party that can produce a record of service to the people . . . the party that is the least partisan and the most patriotic . . .

that party will win. A party that is overly partisan, overly quarrelsome and obsessed solely with politics will lose." [29]

Political parties came into existence because they were needed and persist today because they are still needed. Persons who disregard or minimize their importance have a warped picture of their role in politics and government. A clergy friend of many years, Ray Wallace of the state of Oklahoma, who really never has been antagonistic toward political parties but never an active participant either, shared these views with the readers of his weekly column for a national church weekly: ". . . the erosions of time have forced on me a conclusion I cannot ignore: the complexities of existence are so varied that it is doubtful whether change in society can be accomplished without conspicuous involvement in partisan politics." [30] If my friend's observation has merit, and I believe it does, the status of political parties in America is of immense importance to persons of religious convictions.

The Status of Political Parties

The status of American political parties is transitory, for the position and role of parties constantly change. Any description can be quickly outdated. Whether these changes are the cause or the consequence of the apparent reduction of party influence in American political life is debatable. That the parties are weaker is measurable quantitatively through election returns, public opinion polls, and party affiliation trends. Qualitatively the chaotic condition of many governmental efforts at all levels raises a legitimate question: Who's running the show? If the parties are running the show, they must be held accountable. If they are not running the show, who has taken over and to whom are "they" responsible?

Many foreboding statements are being made about the plight of political parties in America. Professor Everett C. Ladd, Jr. insists that there has been a "pronounced weakening of American political parties . . . in recent decades—a process that . . . has brought them to the point of virtual death as organizations." [31] He contends that parties no longer perform unique functions and that the whole political system has been rattled.

Political parties are supposed to provide a mechanism for the nomination of candidates who, once in office, plan, organize, and implement governmental policies reflective of the wishes of the majority who put them in office but directed toward the universal good of the total populace. To accomplish these ends the allegiance of their members is necessary if parties are to control their own destinies. In recent years the trend away from party affiliation, and movements within both major parties to weaken inner control of party machinery, has resulted in weaker parties. "They have become," as Ladd reminds us, "an endangered species, and an all-out campaign ought to be launched to protect and revive them." [32]

Decline in party affiliation is a fact of our time. Those who classify themselves as political independents rose from 17 percent in 1937 to 31 percent in 1977. The greatest loss was suffered by the Republican party which declined from 34 percent in 1937 to 20 percent in 1977. The Democratic party remained relatively stable with 49 percent in 1977 compared to 48 percent in 1937.

But neither party has held the allegiance of its members. Recent studies observe that throughout American history, most voters have been straight-ticket voters. Until World War II more than 80 percent were so classified. Through the 1950s this statistic remained around 60-70 percent. Of those voting in the presidential race of 1952, 66 percent voted a straight ticket. In 1956 the percentage dropped to 61 percent. A great contrast is presented by George Gallup's 1968 post-election study; he found that only 43 percent of the American voters said they had voted a straight party ticket. More than half of those voting said they had split their ticket. The upward trend of ticket-splitting has continued since 1968 as evidenced by the landslide for President Nixon in 1972 when only 26 percent of the population identified themselves with his party. The 1976 presidential election results do not show as great a percentage of ticket-splitting nationally, but a state-by-state analysis reveals the ticket-splitter has become a rather permanent fixture in American voting behavior. Party loyalties no longer matter to an increasing number of persons, and the end result is a weaker party organization.

There are reasons for this decline in party participation. For one thing, the lack of objectivity prevalent in many party organizations turns many persons off. One author observes that "the ignorance of voters is what makes party government possible." He suggests ". . . a party organization which holds its workers by explicit appeals to issues is, in effect, acting to reduce the ignorance of the voters." [33] It is just such parties that increasingly will be required if rank and file Americans are to accept party affiliation. Each year the American society becomes more highly educated and issue-oriented. The rise in the number of independents is partly due to the refusal of persons to accept clichés that appeal to emotions and bypass truth.

Others turn away from participation because it is boring and filled with endless routine. Local political meetings usually have more to do with patronage questions, political careers of ward leaders, and petty rivalries with neighboring political organizations than with the issues of the day. Frequently the excitement that occurs in a local political organization revolves around a split between two local political leaders (usually over personality differences, not over issues) or as a consequence of a fund raising activity. The political tasks of precinct, ward and township organizations involve the tedious labor of knocking on doors, making phone calls, passing out literature at a plant gate or a supermarket, stuffing envelopes, or getting a crowd to "make a good show" at a political rally. All these activities are necessary and probably inevitable, but are so boring and filled with routine that political participation becomes repulsive to many persons.

The restriction of personal freedom to choose candidates and issues keeps some from political party participation. If a party does not go along with an individual member's choice of a candidate or issue, that member may become dissatisfied. This is especially true for the purist who insists on perfection in each candidate and on every issue. Party strength is not sustained when dissatisfied members desert a party's candidates or issues. The person who recognizes the importance of working within party structures sometimes has difficult choices to make.

Akin to the decline in party membership and affiliation is the reduction in the power of political parties to influence governmental decisions. Unless a political party is able to demonstrate that it can change the course of government, it will cease to be. As indicated previously, the key to politics is power, the power to determine who gets what, when, where and how. A political party has to be able to deliver.

At the local level in America there has been a significant decrease of political party influence in local governments. For good or for naught, an increasing number of local governmental bodies are elected in nonpartisan elections. Across the country, "citizen groups" have come into existence to displace "corrupt" partisan politics. Although these groups are usually the legitimate offspring of politically sensitive persons who conceived them to be their only means of cleaning up a bad situation, the resulting link of "partisan politics" with "corruption" is unfortunate. When conscientious persons in a community identify with the political party of their choice and labor within its organization, there is less corruption; the cleansing by a nonpolitical group may not be needed.

At the state and national level, the advent of mass communications has ushered in an era where individual candidates dominate the political scene. Party labels mean less and less in terms of being elected. As a consequence, once elected, a media-oriented candidate feels little loyalty to his party. Many statewide and national officeholders view political party officials and party persons more to be endured than to be heard for their views on critical governmental issues.

The problems of political parties do not end with disregard of their leaders by officeholders. At the lowest level in the political pecking order, the political patronage job is almost an anachronism. Persons in politically appointed positions frequently feel they must justify or apologize for their jobs. The assumption is hastily made that merit jobs are good and patronage jobs are bad.

Such views are based on the false premise that "merit" can be easily and fairly identified and rewarded exactly as it ought to be. An equally false premise is that "patronage" is inherently evil and always an unsavory political payoff. Overlooked is the very real factor that human beings with human failings as well as human virtues are involved in both "merit" and "patronage" employment. In my own governmental experience I have observed instances of a patronage use of merit as well as the meritorious use of patronage.

The facts are that few political appointees feel the disinterest in the voters that many merit or civil service appointees do. As election day approaches, the political appointee feels the tingle of electoral excitement. He knows that on election day his performance is going to be evaluated. But the merit or civil service appointee feels no pressure to perform, and frequently cannot be gotten rid of if he does not do a good job.

It may be worthwhile to temper the flaws of political appointees by bringing in a reasonable number of civil servants to work along with them. By the same token, it may be worthwhile to temper the civil servants with political appointees. By mixing the two groups, the strengths of each may be used to produce the best possible government.

But that kind of mix does not exist today, and both the political parties and the general public are the poorer. Sometimes I think those who consider themselves to be the most intellectual and thoughtful are really the most biased and unthinking. Religiously sensitive citizen-politicians can bring a refreshing view to this subject if they are determined to be bound neither by the purist attitudes of the sophisticates, who see nothing redeeming in any patronage selection, nor by the naive assumption of many political types that jobs are more important to a party than the loyalty of those who participate in party affairs for what they can give.

The status of American political parties is not encouraging. Unfortunately, as one commentator on politics has observed, "Men can be elected in the United States in part because they are NOT politicians, and because they are thought to be 'above politics.'

Politics is seen to be an ugly realm of scheming, of calculation, of compromise, of general nastiness." This widespread public hostility, or at least apathy, toward politicians and political parties hampers their ability to function well. Negativism is seldom the creative author of anything worthwhile. A more positive attitude toward the role of political parties in American government must be developed for the preservation of a truly democratic form of government.

Much of what passes these days for laudable abstinence from unsavory political participation is really the outward evidence of political apathy and neglect. To be independent is the goal of many well-meaning citizens who, if they were honest with themselves, would recognize their independent aspirations for what they are—an unwillingness to be involved in the urgently needed task of making political parties relevant and responsible.

I do not mean to be too hard on independents. There are many conscientious persons who make a conscious and deliberate choice to participate politically as independents. In their judgment they can be most effective as independents and may, for reasons of their own, be intellectually and ethically uncomfortable participating in a political party. There are times and places when effective political action is not possible within the available party structures. Under such circumstances the way of the independent is the only way available. But the decision as to whether to participate in a political party should be a deliberate decision.

It is unfortunate a greater emphasis is not placed on political party participation by religious groups. I recall searching through a booklet, put out by my denomination as a guide to political action, for directions on how to become involved and effective in a political party. The booklet, entitled "Register Citizen Opinion," begins by asking: "Do you, as a citizen of the United States, hope to exert meaningful influence on public affairs? Do you seek to relate effectively moral values to national issues? Then you have a responsibility to register your opinion with the persons making the decisions before they are made." The booklet is well done and helpful except there is no mention of gaining effectiveness within a political party as a basic means for registering citizen opinion. This is undoubtedly just an oversight, but the low profile political parties occupy among religious groups contributes to the continuation of such neglect.

Other groups with causes work through political parties. Perhaps religiously sensitive persons can learn lessons from them and utilize the political parties instead of resorting to modern alternatives.

Modern Alternatives to Political Parties

It is inevitable when political parties fail, for whatever reasons, to meet the political needs which brought them into being, that alternative methods and organizations are utilized by an anxious public. Persons concerned with the level of religious influence in American politics are obligated to consider any alternative that shows promise of assisting in mixing religion and politics. Out of such consideration may come a new appreciation of the untapped potential of political parties or, what is more likely, ideas as to how political party participation can be effectively supplemented.

One obvious alternative is the issue-oriented movement or organization. These generally fall into one of two categories: (1) broad-based, publicly oriented or (2) special interest. An example of the first is Common Cause, a broad-based citizens group that came into being after the Watergate events to gain greater citizen involvement in a wide range of issues, beginning with reform of political party organizations and campaign spending. An example of the second is any group seeking governmental benefits for their particular interest: Farm Bureau, National Farmers Organization, etc. for farmers, American Medical Association for physicians, National Manufacturers Association for management, AFL-CIO for labor, etc. Millions of Americans are more comfortable expressing their political concerns through such groups than through participation in political parties.

It is interesting that historically, in this nation, groups of this type have not evolved into viable political parties. Other nations, such as France and Germany, have had numerous issue-oriented parties, but in the United States, issue parties have never been very strong. Through the years, statutes in various states and at the national level have been tilted to favor a two-party political system. But the issue movements continue as attractive alternatives to political party participation for many Americans.

A second alternative is the packaged candidate. Millions of Americans proudly exclaim they "vote for the man, not the party." Their knowledge of the man (or woman) is secured not from a political party but from the image-makers, the TV political ad producers, the public opinion pollsters, and a host of other personages devoted to selling a candidate like a merchant sells his wares. The public may get a good public official or it may get a lemon. Regardless of the outcome, an increasing number of persons select their candidate like they buy their groceries at the supermarket—the most attractive package gets their vote, regardless of what political party or social or commercial forces are marketing the package.

Political parties frequently choose the candidate who can be made into the most attractive package to run on their ticket. The candidate who can win, even if he cannot govern, is more important to some within the parties than the candidate who is more difficult to elect but known for his ability to govern.

Widespread governmental social programs are chosen by many as an alternative to political parties. In days when life was not so complex, the ward and precinct political party worker was frequently a social worker as well as a political leader. Today those functions have been displaced by mammoth government participation in welfare, housing, health, and other social services. There is less dependence on political parties to deliver needed social services. Millions of Americans in the lower socio-economic levels, who formerly sought material aid from political parties, no longer have this need for political party involvement.

The growing popularity of direct primary elections is an alternative that lessens the pressure for persons to participate in a political party. When candidates are picked by popular vote in a primary election instead of by the party convention, the party is weakened because victory for a candidate depends more on popular appeal and less on party activity. The real negative feature is that in these days of the packaged candidate, as noted above, the candidate with the greatest public appeal may not be the candidate best equipped to serve if elected.

A particularly disturbing trend is the growing number of states holding direct primaries to elect delegates to the parties' national presidential nominating conventions. Theoretically this sounds great, especially to idealistic persons. It is claimed "the people" instead of the politicians make the choice. But actually the image-makers may gain more power at the expense of responsible political party involvement.

In 1976 I was thrilled to be elected, in a very open, democratic process, as a delegate from my congressional district to the Democratic National Convention in New York. At the convention, I received an even greater thrill when I was elected Chairman of the Missouri delegation. There my thrills ended. The decision to nominate Jimmy Carter had already been made in the primaries. We tried to debate the platform, but those decisions had already been made by the platform committee. Procedural rules adopted previously (at the 1972 convention) made changes and even meaningful objections impossible. Microphones had been installed in Madison Square Garden at great expense for the chairman and members of each state's delegation. They were used but twice—once to announce the state's vote (already predetermined in the thirty-odd states with presidential primaries) for the presidential nomination and then again to announce the votes for the vice-presidential choice (already made by Jimmy Carter).

My point is that party leaders have little to do and less to say when party responsibility for nominating candidates is taken away. I do not believe the ultimate result is in the people's best interest. If a party's leadership is to be held responsible for how its candidates serve as public officials—and they should be held responsible—then they deserve the right to participate meaningfully in the selection process.

A final alternative, and there are many others not mentioned in these pages, is the trend toward public financing of political campaigns. While I favor this movement, it is not without its negative effects on political party participation. "He who pays the piper calls the tune." Once the financing of candidates is removed from the political parties, it becomes increasingly difficult for the party to have input into government, even through its own elected officials. Unfortunately, this possibility is also present when the financing of candidates comes largely from special interest groups and/or wealthy individuals who then become the pipers who call the tune.

All these alternatives to party involvement have certain meritorious features. But to the extent that persons permit these alternatives to displace their participation in political parties, they are unfortunate. The rationale for political party participation which follows may help to highlight why religiously sensitive citizen-politicians are needed in political parties.

A Rationale For Political Party Participation

The picture appears dismal. Persons who feel compelled to become politically involved because of convictions that their religious faith requires such involvement may despair of political party participation once they get a taste of it. After the newness wears off, people who enthusiastically plunged into the political stream may head for the shore for fear of drowning in unfamiliar waters. They may ask if there is not a better way to mix religion and politics then through the laborious plodding of political party activities. They may conclude that it just does not make sense to engage in activities and go through motions that seem so irrelevant to achieving the personal and social goals to which religion causes them to aspire. But it *does* make sense. There are two basic reasons why religiously sensitive persons should choose to be active participants in a political party.

First, the American political party offers the best possibility for effective participation in the political process. Many times I hear

Former Congressman James Symington speaks at a fund raising dinner for James Spainhower.

people say, "I want to make my efforts count where the action is really taking place." I tell them to get active in their political party for there is plenty of action there, and they can make a difference through their participation in its affairs.

Those who are basically ideological persons will be attracted to issue groups and may feel they ought to join an issue-based party. Although they may recognize that issue-based parties have never been effective in this nation, they may also rationalize that they must go with a group in whose principles they believe. The fuzziness of America's major parties on so many issues repels many persons of strong convictions.

In her study of Lyndon Johnson, Kearns observed that "what the critics saw as 'defects' in the party system—its fuzziness and its fragmentation—he saw as virtues. That fuzziness, he contended, was not simply a political expedient, but an authentic reflection of the American people's own ambiguities of conviction and purpose, . . ." [34] If religion and politics are to be mixed, it will not be accomplished by persons who remain outside the structures that have been created to house the political aspirations of the American people. In spite of the fact that many of us are fleeing these structures for independent existence, religiously sensitive citizen-politicians must not join the flight. Those who are willing to accept responsibility for the direction of society are needed within the party structures.

The political party movement in the United States, in spite of the prevailing pessimism concerning its viability, continues for most of us as a potential means for making an impact on politics today. I do not believe that we Americans, notwithstanding our brisk negative comments, have given up on the parties. Persons who come from a religious heritage surely can feel at home in political parties that must thrive on ideals unrealized, hopes unfulfilled, and trust sometimes unreturned.

I have referred to David Broder's masterful offense on behalf of the political party movement because he writes so eloquently and clearly about what must be done if political parties are to regain lost glamor and shine with new resolve. Broder is right, as are others who believe political party neglect must be stopped. Unfortunately, as Broder writes, "the fact is that in the last two decades it is only the insiders—those already heavily involved in politics and government—who have given a damn about the health or sickness of the party system." [35]

The political party offers religious persons the opportunity to go on the offensive. The alternatives to political parties discussed earlier in this chapter have more appeal for those in retreat than they do for persons who want to get things done. Through political participation, religiously sensitive citizen-politicians can be involved in the labors of an umbrella group that can bring together issue-oriented persons and groups, special interests, diverse ethnic groups, and rank-and-file citizens in pursuit of the common interest. The very diversity of a political party makes it fascinating and enticing to those with a thirst for involvement.

The problem in all this talk about effectiveness as a party member is that many religious persons steadfastly refuse to tie themselves down to one party. I understand this reluctance but insist it must be overcome. No party will fit philosophical or political needs entirely; just as few find any one religious faith that satisfies them in every respect. But if religious persons believe there is a God and that he needs religious groups to carry out his work on earth, they will join the group that most nearly expresses their religious faith.

There are at least four contributions such persons can make to political parties.

First, with their background and interest in ethics, religious persons can help political parties consider the ethical aspects of their positions and practices. Most party leaders and members do not want to engage in unethical acts or support activities that will weaken the moral fiber of the nation. But they frequently will do either or both unless there are those among their ranks who are willing to point out the unethical nature of the proposed course of action. The religiously sensitive citizen-politician makes this contribution not so much by what he says but by the kind of person he is and by what he does.

Second, religious persons can be a positive influence in preventing political parties from letting their political power propel them into unwise actions. As a legislator, I have seen my party in the Missouri state legislature, strutting proudly with its lopsided majority, enact laws that were foolish and raise or cut appropriations needlessly merely to demonstrate it had the power to do so. There are 163 members in the Missouri legislature, so 82 members constitute a majority. Members of my party used to talk about Rule 82—you can do anything you want as long as you get 81 other members to agree. Governors were "shown," programs were eliminated, and appropriations were cut to demonstrate that my party had the power and was willing to use it. Religiously sensitive legislators can help prevent such irresponsible actions from taking place if they are trusted party members.

Third, religious persons can be a positive influence in keeping political campaigns on a high level. The public is alienated from the political process not only by dishonesty in money matters but also by campaign practices and rhetoric that are blatantly offensive. The person who has proved his interest in the party will be heard when, for the success of the party, he appeals for higher level campaigns.

Fourth, the restoration of public confidence in political parties can be given a needed boost by politically active religious persons. Such persons must first be the kind of persons who earn a good name among their peers. Then they must become politically active. If truly good persons are willing to be identified publicly with political parties, the general public will be encouraged to trust the parties with significant public responsibilities.

In the area of raw politics, both major political parties sometimes act as if the end goal of a political party is to win elections—period. Such a shortsighted goal may mean temporary political victories, but the long-term prospects for any party that permits itself to be guided by such mistaken logic are disastrous.

The end of it all—of active participation in the political process —is to demonstrate that, as Thomas Jefferson put it in the Declaration of Independence, "It is man's natural right to govern himself." If people refuse to do what by nature they are expected to do, then they shall soon lose their natural capacity for self-government.

There is an understandable tendency to become worn out with the endless stream of political oratory about the virtues of self-government, and the urgings to take a more active part in the democratic process sometimes seem trite. But irritation with such pleadings to become political is dangerous. Those who are willing to let others tend their political gardens and mold their political aspirations will end up without political substance, political vitality, or political freedom. They will be prisoners of their own making, and before they know it, they will have lost the capacity to govern themselves.

When persons are active members of a political party, they cannot escape public involvement that will provide them with the exercise necessary to prevent personal political decay. When their party wins an office, their labors are not over.

In 1832 a United States senator from New York, William L. Marcy, stood on the floor of the United States Senate and uttered some words whose thesis is widely accepted. Said Senator Marcy: "To the victor belongs the spoils." At least in the minds of the general public, victory for a political party conjures up visions of choice political plums in the form of patronage jobs.

It cannot be denied that the victors receive a certain amount of honor and prestige and appointments which fall into the category of political plums. But, a more accurate statement than Senator Marcy's "to the victors belong the spoils" is this: "To the victors belong the *toil*."

The party that wins the control of government, the victorious candidates and their political appointees, does not by the mere fact of victory at the polls inherit a sweet situation where "never is heard a discouraging word and the skies are not cloudy all day." Instead, they receive a mandate to toil diligently, earnestly, honestly, and responsibly in the tremendous by important work of government.

The famous Kentucky legislator, Henry Clay, declared in 1829 that "government is a trust" and years later President Grover Cleveland based his conduct of the office of the presidency upon the idea that "a public office is a public trust." A winning political party, after it has savored its victory, must get to work quickly. To the victors belong the toil on behalf of the people, and for the good of the people.

The party that fails to win control does not escape responsibility in a democracy. It has a watchdog role as the out-of-office party. There are many splendid opportunities for religious persons to influence government positively and constructively as members of a defeated minority party. The action may not be as glamorous as that of the majority party, but if carried out carefully, is frequently of great value.

The illustrations of responsible minority party activity of officeholders are numerous. During and before World War II, Senator Arthur Vandenburg, Republican of Michigan, assisted in keeping America's foreign policy on target through his bipartisan support of a Democratic administration's international relations. As Majority Floor Leader of the Democratically controlled Senate, Lyndon Johnson was of immeasurable assistance to the Republican administration of Dwight Eisenhower. The Panama Canal treaties, with their requirement of a two-thirds vote by the Senate, would never have been ratified without the courageous pro-stand of the Minority Floor Leader, Howard Baker of Tennessee.

Non-officeholding members of the minority party can function within their own sphere of activity as responsible and loyal opposition. By their words and actions they can take to task fellow party members who are irresponsible in their opposition. Frequently minority party activists disregard the overriding concern every party must have for the public good. They measure every action of those in power in terms of how it can be used to restore them and their party to power. Religiously sensitive citizen-politicians can be the leveling common sense influence that prevents a party from being overcome by such madness.

The truth is that cynicism about politics and government must be overcome if both are to be responsive and responsible. The starting place for persons who want to make a responsible use of political parties is to choose the one within which they feel they can work. It is at this point religiously sensitive persons, especially of the purist type, have difficulty. They cannot go along with many of the views and activities of either party so they refuse to become involved. They cannot understand that no one in a political party agrees all the time with what his party says or does. They do not realize that American political parties are too diverse in their composition for rigid ideology.

Although I am a staunch member of my own Democratic party, there are many Republicans with whose views I feel more comfortable than I do with positions taken by some of my fellow Democrats. Further, at various levels, my party takes positions or uses tactics with which I am in total disagreement while Republicans may take stands and use tactics in accord with my own views. But in the main, I am more "at home" with Democrats, so that is where I labor politically.

When it comes to voting, I believe in straight-ticket voting as much as conscience will permit. There are times when a party puts up a candidate who challenges straight-ticket loyalties. In such cases, each voter must weigh carefully for whom he will vote. Each person must judge for himself if there is justification for ticket-splitting. As a general rule, though, government is stronger when one party is clearly in the dominant leadership position and can be held responsible.

One possible advantage of split-ticket voting is its reminder to political parties that the public will not tolerate weak candidates or candidates who are radically different from the center. The point is not that the center position is morally right or wrong; the point is that the majority of Americans are in the center and a political party, to lead effectively, must not stray too far from the center.

It may be helpful to make some practical suggestions about how to become active in a political party. First, the decision must be made as to which party to join. I suggest either the Republican or Democratic party for reasons discussed earlier regarding the relative ineffectiveness of issue-oriented parties in our political life. With few exceptions, the political parties given responsibility for governing in this country are the two major ones.

Parties in most states are organized according to provisions outlined by state law. These laws usually provide for an organizational structure that begins with the selection in a primary election of a Party Committeeman and a Party Committeewoman at the ward or township level. These persons are the official representatives of their party at the local level.

Find out who your committee persons are, contact them, tell them you want to become active, and prove you are serious by attending the next ward or township meeting. Most wards, townships, or counties have regular meetings open to all interested party members in their area. As a regular participant in these gatherings, religious persons will soon find opportunity to assume political responsibilities at the local level. When elections are held, there will be many ways to be active. Gradually religiously sensitive citizen-politicians will become one of the group with influence commensurate to their interest, ability, and political judgment.

From time to time there will be issues or candidates religious persons may want to encourage their local group to support or oppose. They may decide to bring such matters to the agenda of their group personally. In time, as religious persons become more knowledgeable and experienced, opportunities for political party involvement beyond the local level will present themselves. They may want to become candidates themselves. But the place to begin with personal participation is in the organization or group of the political party in the local area.

What many citizens cannot fathom is that one can be a loyal party member without being narrow and exclusive in one's views and social relationships. I frequently point out to my Republican friends that Republicans make great wives, fathers, and fathers-in-law. My wife *was* a Republican as was my deceased father. My father-in-law persists as a loyal Republican and I am proud of him for it. Party membership is not to shut us out of our natural relationships; it is to include us within the activities of a political group very necessary to effective government.

The party isn't over! Persons of religious faith are needed by each party, whether or not the party realizes it. Men and women of unquestioned integrity and sincere dedication to high principles are a breath of fresh air for political parties at every level of their existence!

5

Stay in the Kitchen

"If you can't stand the heat, stay out of the kitchen," President Harry S Truman is credited with saying. He used the phrase many times to warn of the trials certain to plague any holder of public office.

It is not only on persons in elected positions that pressures become intense. Any official, elected or appointed, responsible for the administration of the public's business, must be prepared to hear from the people. And the people are not always polite or even fair. These are days when cynicism toward politicians runs rampant throughout society.

These are days when much of the general public is discouraged, disillusioned, and disgusted with the manner in which public affairs are conducted, and a large number of public officeholders are leaving office with similar feelings.

What has happened to this nation? Do we no longer believe that democracy works? Are we no longer convinced that government of the people, by the people and for the people is a realistic way of addressing and solving our common problems?

One of the men I most admire in Missouri politics did not run for reelection in 1976. After twelve years in Congress, my friend, William Hungate, said he "lost passion for public office." In making his announcement not to seek reelection, Congressman Hungate reported that "under the weight of frustrated hopes, unreasonable pressures and the job's persistent demands, my enthusiasm for public service waned."

Hungate then made this very incisive observation: "In the last decade, politics has gone from the age of 'Camelot,' when all things were possible, to the age of 'Watergate,' when all things are suspect."

Although the age of Camelot is identified in the public mind with the administration of the late John F. Kennedy, the mental inhabitants of this age are to be found in every administration. They are those who think that all things are possible. They are those who believe that if we can put one of our own kind on the moon—if human technology can do that—then technology can accomplish anything.

Illusions persist with permanent residence in Camelot! Such illusions include the belief that environmental problems will be solved in a generation, that lasting peace among the nations is just a step away, that the energy problem is subject to immediate solution, that soon people will learn how to distribute food on the basis of need; and that the eradication of disease is imminent!

In the age of Camelot it is acceptable to believe that civil rights for all is just around the corner, that the removal of governmental oppression and human poverty from the face of the globe is near; and that the demise of selfishness from the body and spirit of all will soon come to pass. Hope does spring eternal in us and never more so than in the age of Camelot.

So laws are passed, the programs are formulated, and like a mighty army the citizens of the age of Camelot move forward against the foes! Admittedly and thankfully, some of these obstacles to human happiness and prosperity will fall before the onslaught of united human endeavor. Others, however, will stand, because immediate victory is not to be had even in the age of Camelot.

Where, then, shall the people find strength to face difficult days? When the spirit is vanquished, how can the glory of a past be resurrected for the living of a new day? Were not the dreams of the age of Camelot dreams that people ought to have? Were they not just and fair and visionary in the tradition of those who aspire for the best? How can they fail when they are so right?

Well, the truth is that the dreams and aspirations of all of history's ages of Camelot have not totally failed. It was in the spirit of Camelot that George Washington fathered a nation. It was in the spirit of Camelot that Thomas Jefferson wrote the Declaration of Independence and oversaw the purchase of the Louisiana Territory.

It was in the spirit of Camelot that Abraham Lincoln laid the foundations for the beginning of freedom for every black person in America. It was in the spirit of Camelot that Albert Schweitzer provided for the medical and spiritual needs of thousands of black

Africans from his humble jungle hospital. It was in the spirit of Camelot that Teddy Roosevelt helped break the hold of great monopolies over the economic life of America.

It was in the spirit of Camelot that Woodrow Wilson envisioned a worldwide organization of nations where the representatives of the world could discuss their mutual problems with words instead of fighting them out with bullets. Woodrow Wilson's vision was not attained in his time and is not yet a complete reality, but because he dared to dream, the world is closer to achieving Wilson's ideals than it otherwise would have been.

It was in the spirit of Camelot that Franklin Roosevelt succeeded in delivering this nation from fear, and as a result of his dreams, America does a better job of living up to its ideals than was the case before this man appeared on the scene. It was in the spirit of Camelot that Harry Truman refused to accept the insolvency of the post-war world as being inevitable, and through his efforts the Marshall Plan helped to restore the economic balance needed for the economic health of all mankind.

Although John Kennedy never lived to see it, his emphasis on the need for a new spirit of Camelot in the United States continues to inspire millions of persons to take their obligations of citizenship more seriously.

The age of Camelot always has its successes, but never does it have all successes. Its danger is that people may come to accept it as an accurate portrayal of what society is instead of a blueprint for what society must ever strive to become. And society will never begin to reach its potential until religiously sensitive persons are willing to get into the kitchen of political activity and stay there.

To stand for election to public office or to accept appointment to a public position gets a person into the kitchen where the heat is. Because the financial rewards are not all that great, unless individuals are sensitive to appeals to their conscience to do their public duty, or are possessed by large egos that delight in being in the public eye, or are the type who thrive on being in a position of power and decision-making, they may refuse to stay in the public kitchen.

Religiously sensitive citizen-politicians should not make such refusals. They should stay in the kitchen, run for office, accept appointment to office, or help candidates in whom they believe.

Persons of religious convictions are frequently discouraged from running for office because of a widespread belief, voiced succinctly years ago by President Franklin D. Roosevelt's long-time companion and personal secretary, Louis M. Howe, that "you can't adopt politics as a profession and remain honest." Or, as the English poet Edward Young observed, "The public path of life is dirty."

President Jimmy Carter tells of the advice he received from a minister not to become involved in a "discredited profession" and instead, as the minister put it, "If you want to be of service to other people, why don't you go into the ministry or into some other honorable social service work?"[36]

This attitude that political service is inevitably dishonest, discredited, and a lower form of social service resides within many parents. Some fathers and mothers are called wise, and consider themselves wise, when they advise their young: "Whatever you do, don't get mixed up in politics."

There are few experiences more heartening than to share the trials of a candidate in whom you have faith and, conversely, there are few disappointments any greater than that of having a politician betray your trust. The political process has been deeply wounded in recent years by what Theodore White calls a "breach of faith." To enlist persons of either or no political party in the support of a political candidate has been extremely hampered by the sad events and revelations of the past few years. For all too many Americans, the thrill of supporting a candidate has been dealt a staggering blow. If once again Americans are to thrill in their politics, there must be a new order of politicians who take seriously the ethical demands of their calling.

This new order of politicians will not be able to survive either the cynicism of the past, nor the jungle-like atmosphere of present political struggles for power, without the support of Americans whose involvement in the political process goes beyond casting a ballot on election day. Religious persons running for office must be in the forefront of this new order.

One of the impediments for such persons is the assumption voiced by numerous persons that holders of elective office generally are warped persons not quite like normal persons. In recent years there have been many books and articles on the actual or assumed deviate behavior of politicians. Revelations of extra-marital affairs by former Presidents and incidents of sexual promiscuity among current officeholders has encouraged the general public to believe that it really takes a socially abnormal person to serve in public office. Even so prestigious a newspaper as *The Wall Street Journal* was led to editorialize on the subject of "Sex and Politics" when the sexual practices of some members of Congress became public knowledge. The editors of the *Journal* concluded that if "sexual misbehavior is in fact far more common and more flagrant among politicians than among ordinary Americans . . . There will be reason to wonder about the type of man attracted to public life."[37] With such a foreboding prospect, religious persons hesitate to run for office, especially when they ponder this question asked by the editorial just noted: "Is there something in this process—the type of ambition required to stand for office, the temptation to indulge in pretense, the necessity to manipulate people, the clubbish tolerance of the peers you find in office—that in the end warps character?"[38] No one wants to be classified as some sort of human freak. Public perceptions of politicians, fueled by the unfortunate antics of some politicians, and the sweeping generalities of commentators, discourage many persons from running for office.

It is natural to seek the easy way of getting a job accomplished. This quest for simple solutions appeals to persons who want to reorder society along more ethical lines without personally having to run for office. Reluctance to run for and serve in public office is understandable on grounds other than these.

Any who serve or have served in public office know it is impossible to be a politician without some of the muck and mire of the political process rubbing off on them. The stains of political encounters are not pretty but they are real and inevitable. They are part of the price paid for the thrills of political service. There is no hypocrisy greater than that of the politician who presents himself as above and beyond contamination by politics. The best that can be done is to keep reminding persons that the high public purposes which politics at its best strives to achieve are worth the disgusting political encounters that frequently cannot be escaped. These encounters often involve a politician in experiences that do not thrill him.

For instance, I am not thrilled by the number of office-seekers and officeholders who sustain themselves with bolstered egos which so easily accompany running for or serving in public office. For these people it becomes heady stuff to be wined, dined, and flattered day in and day out.

A certain amount of ego can be invaluable, in that it builds and sustains confidence—and confidence is a key ingredient in successfully administering a public office. But when ego becomes the primary force moving the life of an elected official, the business of government is relegated to a subordinate position. No man or woman can serve an inflated ego and the public welfare at the same time.

Nor am I thrilled by the slick maneuvers of self-serving politicians whose concept of public service is that public offices exist to serve them and their private political ambitions instead of the public good. If success in politics requires a man to develop the art of personal deception and self-deluding illusions of power and importance, persons cannot be blamed for refusing to seek office.

There can be, and for the religious person must be, higher motivations for seeking elective office. Chief among those motivating factors must be the conviction that ultimately government is honorable because honorable people agree to serve in public office. It must become an article of faith that even one truly good person in public office strengthens society. People have to become convinced that persons of integrity, by their very presence in a public office, hold out hope that society can govern itself with decency, dignity and honor.

There are so many instances of corruption in public office that it is no wonder cynicism about running for office pervades and causes persons who ought to be in charge of public affairs to refuse to run for office. Frequently persons suggest corruption exists because of an imperfect system. They then conclude the way to dispose of corruption is to reform the system.

But, as *The Kansas City Times* once said in an editorial: "No reforms, however sweeping, can guarantee purity in government. That depends on the integrity and fiber of individuals. Laws can set the guidelines, but in the final analysis behavior is a matter of personal conscience and commitment."[39]

Although religious persons may believe those words—it is an awfully big step to run for office! It is much more comfortable to "let George do it." But now and then, here and there, some must be willing to take the name of George and go into the kitchen. What follows is especially for those "Georges" and for others who want to be better equipped to assist those Georges.

Pre-filing Suggestions

Many persons mistakenly assume that running for office begins with filing for office. If that is the starting point, the candidate is way behind before he or she begins. My experience has been that too many candidates do not give as much attention to pre-filing matters as they should.

The citizen-politicians who are serious about running for office should first spend considerable time analyzing themselves, their convictions, their temperament, their personal situation.

People's convictions are the bedrock upon which they will build their candidacy and, if they are successful, their later service in public office. It is highly important for potential candidates to be candid with themselves about their motivations for entering politics. Senator Mark Hatfield admits that, for most politicians, ambition and ego motivate their journey in public life. He reveals that he ran for the state legislature not because he wanted to spend his life as a member of Oregon's House of Representatives, but because he thought he could become a State Senator, and then perhaps Secretary of State, and maybe even Governor. As it turned out, he exceeded his highest ambition!

But ambition and ego are not sufficient reasons to enter politics. As Hatfield himself writes, "Political service must be rooted in a philosophy of society's overall well-being, with a broad vision of how the body politic serves the people through its corporate structures. The heart of one's service in the political order must be molded by ideals, principles, and values." [40] President Carter, in an interview during his campaign for the presidency, stated his public service aspirations simply: "I believe God wants me to be the best politician I can possibly be."

During the 1976 campaign, a national news magazine conducted a survey on American leadership. Participants were asked to name three attributes they believed most needed in today's leaders. Moral integrity was listed by 76.1 percent, courage by 55.2 percent, and common sense by 52.9 percent. These responses indicate the desire of a vast majority of the people for officeholders who have moral convictions and possess the courage and common sense to live up to those convictions once elected to office.

Persons need to be very conscious of all aspects of their personal temperament before filing for office. Potential candidates should ask themselves: How do I react under pressure? Can I emotionally handle criticism? Do I really and genuinely like people? Do I enjoy being in crowds? Am I comfortable among strangers? Do I meet people easily? Am I enough of an extrovert to go into new surroundings and immediately proceed to get acquainted with everyone there?

The hard truth must sometimes be faced that a very dedicated and otherwise capable person just is not suited to run for office. The usual purpose of running for office is to win. Only rarely is it worth the effort or wise strategy to seek office knowing the temperament necessary to be a successful candidate is missing. It is possible to change and to overcome some temperamental handicaps but, just as zebras have stripes forever, most persons are, temperamentally, what they are as long as they live. It does little good to berate politics and people for being what they are. Politics occupies a hectic, gregarious arena and if persons are unable to function in such an atmosphere, they should admit it and channel their aspirations to mix politics and religion into other areas. People who become politicians face others who are: demanding of attention, insistent on being heard, self-centered, and inclined to look upon office-seekers as creatures to be endured rather than as would-be public servants to be commended for their altruistic desires.

Individuals thinking about running for office wisely analyze their own personal characteristics to see if they are up to the personal strains that are certain to envelop their lives once they begin their campaign.

There are a number of very personal considerations persons should weigh before filing for office. Foremost among these is the fact that once they file for office, there is very little about their lives and their family that can remain private. Thomas Jefferson contended that "when a man assumes a public trust, he should consider himself as public property."

Candidates for public office have no choice whatsoever in whether they will keep their personal and financial matters secret. They will not because either the law or political realities will compel them to go public. On the national level, and in state after state, almost every year new and more stringent disclosure laws are passed. Officeholders' business dealings before entering office are scrutinized carefully by the press and the opposition party. Their personal lives become open books and even the personal habits of their family members become public fodder.

Prospective officeholders may complain, and even attempt to escape the public glare, but chances of success are few. Some minor offices escape this public exposure, but the higher the political office, the greater the demand for public visibility of the officeholders and their entire life's activities. Persons entering politics must be prepared to live in a goldfish bowl. If they are not willing to do so, they will be miserable and so will their families.

This may be an appropriate place to discuss what has always been a difficult personal consideration for those serving in public office —family attitudes toward the proposed candidacy. Initial reactions of family members may be positive because they want their loved one to do what he or she wants to do or because they, too, share similar concerns. Later, when the campaign gets underway with all its pressures and still later when the office is assumed and begins to make its inevitable demands on time, loyalty, and priorities, the family may resent the political career.

The files of political careers are replete with many instances of divorce, separation, and/or estrangement between marriage partners, and sometimes between officeholders and their parents, or between officeholders and their children. It is not always possible to know in advance what the response of one's family will be. But it is helpful for potential candidates to approach the subject candidly and openly with family members and seek to minimize any negative effects upon family relationships.

A major concern for candidates, especially if they are not independently wealthy, is how to support themselves and their families while running for office. Campaigning for an office that is a full-time position usually requires spending full-time campaigning from three months to a year or a year and a half for the major statewide offices.

In addition, money has to be raised for the campaign. Prospective candidates should face frankly the financial problems posed to themselves, their families. They should have financial plans made because it is generally too late to make them once the campaign begins in earnest. Persons must face up to any potential or real conflicts of interest that will be the consequence of serving in public office. There may be business interests, personal ties, or civic and social memberships that candidates must be prepared to relinquish if elected.

Health is always a consideration. Increasingly, the pace of public officeholders is vigorous, and only persons of stamina can be expected to endure the physical, mental, and emotional strains of holding public office.

A final personal consideration is the effect on the long-range goals for their careers and their lives. Either defeat or success in a political race, in differing ways, affect a person's future. Before filing for office, candidates must be sure, insofar as they can, that they and their careers are prepared to handle the consequences of either victory or defeat.

After persons have engaged in thorough analyses of their convictions, temperament, and other personal considerations, they then need to analyze the political situation in which they find themselves. It is not sufficient for persons to conclude that they would like to run for office and that they can get their personal lives in order. There remain some very practical and tremendously important political considerations.

Basic to these considerations is what office is to be sought. Too many persons want to run for offices for which they are grossly unprepared and/or which they are unlikely to win. It is better to gain experience in a minor office before proceeding to tackle a major one. Further, the "minor offices" are minor in name only. In every public office there are ample opportunities to make an effective mix of one's religious convictions and political concerns.

Several years ago, William Lowe of Mexico, Missouri, retired from the presidency of the A.P. Green Company. He had also served a term as the national president of the United States Chamber of Commerce and was currently chairman of the board of a noted and successful private college. An active churchman, he decided as a matter of both religious and civic commitment, to run for office. This man was capable of being governor or United States Senator and had he filed for either, few, if any, would have felt he was seeking an office beyond the reach of his capacities. Mr. Lowe decided to seek the position of state representative, to become one of one hundred sixty-three persons in Missouri's lower legislative chamber. He did not win his race, but I admired him for being willing, if the people had wanted him, to begin at the bottom.

Persons should give serious consideration to getting into the kitchen of politics at the lower levels and, in many cases, staying there. I can recall arguments made by many of my nationally-oriented professors of political science in the late sixties that our political problems are too mammoth and complex, so nationwide in scope, that for state and local governments to address them is an exercise in futility. We are beginning to learn the hard lesson that they were mistaken. Social and governmental problems cannot be addressed best, if at all, by the federal government. Local school boards, city councils, neighborhood community improvement associations, hospital districts, soil conservation districts, county commissioners, and state legislative bodies are the public instrumentalities through which a growing number of our nation's problems must be solved.

The implications for religiously sensitive citizen-politicians wanting to run for office are obvious: run for office locally; get into your local kitchen!

Whatever office persons decide to seek, another important consideration is on what political party ticket to run. If persons have a record of long and/or active participation in a particular party, the decision will not be difficult. But if they have not been active in a party and feel they can serve in office as a member of either party, they are faced with a decision that probably can be made best on a pragmatic basis. They need to decide which party offers the greatest chances for electoral success.

I recall a newcomer to statewide politics in my state who had not been identified with either party. When asked why he chose the party he did, his reply was quite candid. "If you were going to a theater and there were only two ticket windows and ten people were standing in the line at one window and nobody was in line at the other window, which line would you take?" he asked. As it turned out he was very successful in the party he chose, for it was uncluttered with candidates.

After an individual decides the party on whose ticket he will seek a spot, his next step is to gather support. Usually it is wise to begin with those who are known to be the political leaders of one's party within the geographical or governmental entity in which the office will be contested. Those leaders may or may not be supportive, but regardless, it is never wise to stop with them. A candidate must reach out and contact as many others as possible *before* filing. It is important to make one's candidacy the candidacy of as many others as possible.

Evaluation of the opposition cannot begin too early. The nature of the opposition may even help to determine whether one will run for office. If the incumbent is running for reelection and is perceived to have done a good job, a person may want to reconsider entering the race. But if there is clearly a need for a change, even though the task may be formidable, a person will want to begin early to analyze the opposition, probe for weaknesses, and plan a strategy for victory.

In planning strategy, the question of how much money it takes to conduct a winning campaign should be addressed early. How and if the money can be raised, must also be considered.

During the pre-filing period, prospective candidates need to learn all they can about the responsibilities of the position to be sought. Good intentions, a good reputation, adequate campaign finances, and a willingness to work hard are all invaluable attributes. But a person will not want to run for office unless she knows she can handle the job she seeks.

Once the decision is made to run for office, it still is not time to file. Prospective candidates should begin working the territory, just as traveling salesmen work their assigned areas. They should begin a card file with the names, addresses, telephone numbers, and pertinent personal information about every personal contact made. After meeting new persons, follow-up letters should be written. In these early days, prospective candidates should share with a few new and old acquaintances their aspirations to run for office. They may want to use them as the core of a later campaign organization.

The names of influential organizations within the candidates' areas should be secured. A list of names and addresses of the officers of these organizations should be obtained, and the prospective candidates should seek ways of establishing contact with these groups and their officers.

The prospective candidates should lay plans to become acquainted with the leaders and opinion-molders in their areas. They should not be reluctant to initiate such contacts because of the false assumption that they are "using" these contacts for political purposes. It is no violation of the integrity of human relations to recognize that some persons are in a position to help the candidates achieve their worthwhile goals. To enlist this kind of help makes good sense.

There are undoubtedly many other things prospective candidates can do to good advantage before filing for office. Eventually, though, the time comes to file for office. Too many candidates just go to the proper election official and file. The wiser ones invite friends and supporters to their homes or to public halls, for a pre-filing party or rally. Such events involve candidates' supporters in making the candidacies theirs.

Getting to know the people he will serve, Mr. Spainhower and his wife, Joanne, visit with a constituent.

Campaign Suggestions

Campaigns need to be well thought out, issues isolated, and an adequate budget prepared and underwritten. On the latter point, a caution about going into debt. Unless personally capable of paying off incurred loans, persons should insist that their campaign "pay as it goes." Winners generally can raise funds to pay off campaign debts (although not easily), whereas losers usually have a difficult task getting the money to retire campaign debts.

A campaign should have a sense of movement, of steady progress. The purpose is to peak on election day. If the candidate and his organization work at the campaign every day, gradually expanding both the candidate's circle of supporters and breadth of contacts, the campaign will pick up momentum. If along the way, central issues in the campaign are methodically and repeatedly emphasized, frequently by use of creative and dramatic events involving the candidate, the campaign really will begin to take shape in the public mind.

Essential to any successful campaign is a candidate who recognizes the political value of a handshake, a smile, and a sincere and friendly interest in persons. The aloof candidate who refuses to get out and meet the people, even in these days of reliance on television and radio, is making it extremely difficult to win.

Recent studies of what influences voters show that with the decrease in straight party voting and the increase of ticket-splitting, there is the following order of inputs into the decision-making process of the voters: candidates, issues, party identification, and group affiliations. The candidate—how he or she is perceived to be in the mind of the voter—still occupies the number one position. So the candidate must try to make the most favorable impression possible. This does not mean a candidate will permit himself or herself to be portrayed as possessing qualities or taking stands on issues that are not true. But it does mean he or she will do everything possible within the bounds of what is true, to be presented in the most favorable light.

Voters need to feel a kinship, a closeness with candidates that is of the same nature they feel for close friends. The conviction has to be implanted in voters that they really can trust the candidates to be what they appear to be, believe what they say they believe, and do what they say they will do. The majority of the electorate wants to vote for persons who are high-minded, committed to sound policies and capable of talking sense to voters rather than for candidates who rely on pet slogans, selfish appeals and patently political rhetoric. Voters want officeholders who will carry out their duties, led by their consciences, not by political bosses. If candidates can come across to the voting public in these terms, they will be elected.

Amoral candidates do whatever is necessary to get the voters to have such confidence in them. For the religiously sensitive candidates, the task is not so simple. Religious persons will permit their media advisers, campaign directors, and anyone else working to get them elected to present them *only* as they actually are. To be associated with the perpetration of fraud on the voters is, to a person of religious conviction, as wrong as if they were selling them a defective piece of merchandise—which in fact they would be.

In the long run, candidates are better off not to present false views of themselves or to promise what they know they cannot deliver. There is always a day of reckoning for the dishonest. Wise are the candidates who recognize that the best way to convey to the voters the image of honest, open, conscientious persons is to be honest, open, and conscientious.

The goal of candidates is to have as many of the voters on their side as possible. They may succeed in getting a majority, maybe even a landslide majority like Johnson's in 1964, or Nixon's in 1972, but they will not be able to *keep* the voters on their side unless the voters continue to believe in them. Time and time again the same theme arises—all that religious persons really have going for them in politics is their unrelenting resolve to reflect in political activities what they really believe is important.

Maximum utilization of free media coverage is important in any political campaign. Actually, an article in the news columns of a newspaper or on a television or radio newscast is much more effective than a paid advertisement. Name identification is critical, for, in spite of what has been said about the integrity needs of a candidate, unfortunately many voters decide who they will vote for purely on the basis of which name they recognize. Studies show a high degree of name identification for candidates in the major political races, such as President, United States Senator, and Governor. But for other statewide officers—judgeships, legislators, and nearly all local officials—the voters' ignorance of the candidates is abysmal. The lesson for candidates is clear: get your name known.

In a primary campaign, candidates are in opposition to members of their own party and have to run alone. This is generally a comfortable position for persons who want to be elected because of what they are. In the general election they run on the party's ticket and have responsibilities to their party. This does not mean that candidates have to sacrifice their own principles, but it is probable they will not always agree with the way the party's total campaign (which now includes their candidacy) is being conducted. The religiously sensitive candidates have to remind themselves continually that they do not have a corner on what is right and true and, when it comes to knowledge of political strategy, they are probably the least informed and experienced. Humility is always befitting a person, and in matters of politics, a first-time candidate has a lot to be humble about!

Most persons have a temper. The counsel is sound: do not lose it in a campaign. There may be justification for losing one's temper in a campaign. The opposition may issue false charges, persons in whom trust is placed may double-cross, promises of support may turn out to be hollow, and best intentions may be twisted to make it look as if a candidate is on the side of the devil. But candidates must not lose their temper.

I am not suggesting that candidates surrender the capacity to speak forcefully or refrain from any display of righteous anger. The public must not get the idea that just because candidates stand for decency and honor in public office they can be pushed around. Candidates can stand their ground without displaying an inability to control temper.

Effective campaigns are well-organized campaigns. There is no substitute, absolutely none, for organization in a campaign. Candidates who think that all they have to do is announce their candidacies, get a few dollars together for some political advertisements, and shake a few hands are in for a big surprise. Winning campaigns are organized to the hilt and the organization is not just on paper, although organizing does begin on paper. Until those plans are implemented, however, they are worthless.

In recent American political history, one of the most effective uses of organization was demonstrated in the campaigns of John F. Kennedy. The philosophy and practice followed in his campaigns is instructive for any candidate running for any office. It was a politics of personal participation on a massive scale.

Candidates must never forget that they are candidates. It is their qualifications, their name, their personality, their image which the voters will consider as they decide who will get their votes. Candidates are very much in the center. This is why candidates may develop huge egos. Always in the center of the stage, their names and pictures appearing on television, billboards, and in newspapers and being blared forth on radio, candidates soon become aware that they are news. It is hoped that the candidates are blessed with enough common sense not to take themselves too seriously. Once the campaign is over, especially if they lose, and there are more losers than there are winners, they will fade from the limelight.

During a campaign, candidates should retain control of their campaigns. Even though others give generously of money and time and put their reputations on the line by backing candidates, the candidates literally put themselves, their honor, on the line. They are fools, then, if they willingly let anything happen in the campaign that is contrary either to their sense of what is right and honorable or to their best judgment. If prospective candidates realize they will not be able to control their campaign, they ought not run. Only misery awaits candidates prevented from controlling their own campaigns unless the eternal intervenes and in some miraculous way takes over. Persons of faith must not count out God, but I maintain that God will help but expects persons to take charge of their own lives and do everything they humanly can. After persons do all they can, then they can safely leave the rest to God!

Serving in Office

In every campaign there are technically winners and losers, but actually, persons who run for office never lose, even if not elected. At this point, however, we consider the responsibilities that descend upon those who are elected.

The first responsibility hardly needs to be stated: Religious persons holding public office will be honest. They don't just talk about honesty; they practice honesty. If from the beginning of their service in office, public officials make it clear by their actions that honesty is more than talk, they will be spared many invitations to engage in dishonest activities. Word of officials' honesty has a way of getting around when they refuse to participate in actions that contradict their pronouncements of honesty.

As important as honesty is, alone it is an inadequate instrument for an officeholder. Foremost among the other attributes needed to serve effectively in public office is common sense. Even though I have spent a large portion of my life pursuing a formal education, I am not much of a scholar. I have greater respect for what used to be called good old common sense. The official possessed by this trait will, as in the days of Harry Truman, tell the people not what they want to hear, but what they have a right to know.

Obviously, officeholders with such a philosophy will run full speed forward to face the hardest issues of the day. They will not run away from issues which divide the public. They will not have to check their latest opinion polls before taking a stand. They will *not* refuse to act for fear of public reaction.

This means that officeholders will be both innovative and decisive. The difficulties and complexities of public service will compel them to seek new and more efficient ways of doing their job. These same concerns will be a daily reminder that once all the facts are in and every preparation completed, officials must act. Indecision in a public office can be critical. The events of time literally have run over officials too timid to exercise the powers of the office to which they were elected. Harry Truman believed decisiveness to be essential to effective government. "That's the meaning of government," he said. "If you're in it, you've got to govern. Otherwise you're in the wrong business."

Fear of the electorate keeps some elected officials from being more decisive. It is not always possible to determine what the public wants nor to be certain that what they say they want reflects their thorough consideration of the facts of the situation. For public officials to take action contrary to their best judgment, when they know the public is reacting on the basis of inadequate knowledge, is reprehensible. People elect candidates to lead, to face difficult issues, and to solve pressing problems. If, when elected, persons cannot or will not face these challenges, they no longer deserve to hold office.

If elected officials are to be decisive, confident that they are acting in the public interest, they have to know their jobs, recruit and retain a capable staff, and be searching constantly for more efficient and economical ways to carry out the tasks of their office.

All citizens should spend some time visiting the chambers of their state legislative body. They might find that body considering issues ranging from the regulation of utilities, to drug abuse, to rules concerning the use of farm insecticides, to financing schools, to setting up standards for the architectural profession, to passing on appropriations for air and water pollution. After such an experience, citizens wouldn't doubt the need for competency in public servants.

The place to begin a quest for knowledge regarding an office is with the constitutional and statutory authorization for the office. Sometimes a predecessor in office will share information. Usually it is possible, and advisable, to confer with the holder of the same office in another jurisdiction. Nearly every public office has regional, state, and national organizations of persons holding the same position. These groups generally publish periodicals and other literature that is helpful. Sometimes they conduct orientation conferences for new officeholders.

When I was elected state treasurer for Missouri, I discovered I had been elected to what is essentially a banking position. My previous experience with banks, other than as a customer, had been confined to a three-month period while in high school as custodian of a local bank! This hardly fitted me with the knowledge I needed about the management and investment of billions of dollars annually.

One of my first acts after taking office was to appoint an ad hoc committee of bankers to review the banking operations of the state treasurer's office and recommend any changes they felt should be made. To guard against any banking interest being tempted to make recommendations favorable to them but not the best policy for the state, I resorted to the time-tested and thoroughly American system of checks and balances. On the committee I included natural competitors who would be certain to keep their eyes on each other.

I met with the committee regularly and learned much from its investigations. At the same time, I visited banks of varying size all over the state, observing their operations and "picking the brains" of their officers and operational personnel. I was a frequent customer of the library, reading many books and articles on subjects relevant to my work as treasurer.

As a result of these efforts, I began to learn my new job. But I was fortunate, as are many newly elected officials, to inherit a staff, with few exceptions, that was experienced and qualified.

I dismissed some persons who did not possess the skills needed. I eliminated a few jobs I felt were unnecessary. In a period of a couple of years I felt comfortable, but not complacent, about my ability to do the job I was elected to do. Elected officials must never forget that they are in elective positions and therefore part of the political process. It is not only permissible but desirable that they make full use of all legitimate political tools at their disposal to do the best job possible. As long as there are constitutional provisions for a public office to be subject to the political process, elected officials have no right to transform the office into a nonpolitical position.

Eradication of the practice of politics from the conduct of government is neither possible nor desirable. For any political party or officeholder to suggest otherwise is unfortunate. It is engaging in the worst kind of duplicity to play the political game on one side while denouncing the practice of politics on the other. Sometimes candidates will claim that if elected they will do away with politics in public office. The sound is good, but no matter how good it sounds, doing away with politics in the running of government is impossible so long as human beings are at the controls.

There can be only bitter disappointment for those who swallow the line that democratic government can persist without the practice of politics.

To be a politician—a *good* politician—is something very commendable. It means that power has been acquired to do good for many people. If a person becomes adept in political procedure, situations can be altered that might otherwise present impossible blocks on the road to progress.

Admittedly, there is much that is not right in the practice of politics in America. Neither political virtue nor political malpractice is the exclusive possession of either Republicans or Democrats. Both parties are, from time to time, inhabited by members who manifest both good and bad political traits. But, despite the presence of corruption and the absence of virtue, and vice versa, the prominent place of politics in the processes of government cannot be eliminated.

Those who have never held public office nor sought to delve into the nature of politics in a democracy may fail to comprehend the necessity for politicians to practice politics if they are to serve in the public interest. Conscientious politicians who understand the meaning of politics are much like well-trained horses. They ride with the pack, waiting carefully until the time is right, and then they throw caution to the wind and with all the power and grace they can command, they make their move!

Wise politicians pay tribute to the whims of the populace—they accede to their desires and bias, frequently in opposition to their own wishes and not infrequently in violation of their better wisdom. But when they perceive their time has come to tackle a task in accord with their conscience—they make their move, and all the votes in the world cannot turn their heads.

To be chosen by citizens to serve in any office is a high honor. Individuals who receive the confidence of their peers are fortunate for they have the opportunity to test and see if the ideals of their faith are workable in the political process. If faith involves betting our life there is a God, mixing religion and politics through service in an elective office is giving ourselves to put our faith into practice.

Handling Political Failures

When highly motivated persons offer themselves for public office and are defeated, the personal trauma may be critical. An even more treacherous situation results when strongly religious persons are elected but are incapable of handling their public duties properly or, through no fault of their own, fail to achieve what they set out to accomplish. Unfortunate circumstances can develop when religious persons become disillusioned by the political process and despair of continuing in the role of citizen-politicians because people failed them. Handling political failures is a subject that must not be neglected because, if persons stay involved in politics long enough, they will experience failures.

To be defeated in an election is not a disgrace but usually is a source of discomfort. A defeated candidate once told me that the first few days were the most difficult, but within a month he actually found himself thanking the voters for his defeat! If a candidate puts forth his best effort, runs a clean campaign, and takes stands for which no apology is owed to anyone, yet still does not win, emotional and intellectual adjustment to the defeat will come fairly quickly.

Candidates are frequently the victims of the times or of unusual circumstances or a combination of both. Among politicians a comment used to explain why some are defeated is that their timing was off. Political scientists have debated for years whether great events produce great leaders or great leaders produce great events.

Defeated candidates are well advised to analyze the reasons for their defeat. If they ever run for public office again, having in their head and on paper their conclusions as to why they were defeated will help them conduct a more effective and, possibly, winning campaign. If they do not seek elective office again, knowledge as to why they were not elected helps endure whatever pain of defeat remains.

A more troublesome situation is when persons are elected but fail to do adequate jobs. Failure may be because they have neither the qualifications nor the aptitude for the job and should never have sought the position. Individuals who find themselves in such situations can resign or remain on the job, do the best they can, and by all means, seek help from persons who do know how the office should be conducted.

Still another disturbing failure is for persons to see policies and programs fail which are basic to their being able to conduct the business of their office. Failure of this kind is especially difficult to bear when the cause of the failure is the opposition by the people who elected them. For officeholders to lose the trust and confidence of the people when they feel deeply about the rightness of their stands is difficult to endure.

There are times when elected officials must not permit themselves to follow the people's wishes. It is in such turmoil that what a person really believes is tested. The people will not long endure leadership unresponsive to the majority's will. And, in a democracy, this is as it should be. But religious persons who get into politics must not suffer the illusion that they will win all battles nor that they will always be able to side with the majority. Citizen-politicians are always supporting what really counts when they are true to their deepest convictions. Obedience to one's conscience is the strength religiously sensitive persons receive to endure the failure that may occur when one has said "no" to the crowds but "yes" to one's sense of what is right for that time, and that issue.

Akin to the pain that follows the failure of programs and policies in which a religious person believes is the pain of having persons in whom one believes prove to be untrustworthy. This happens to persons in and out of public life because human beings are fallible. But in all of life's endeavors, in differing degree depending on the situation, trust has to be placed in persons. Bitter is the disappointment when trusted persons betray confidence.

For a person in public office the repercussions of a betrayal may be extensive and enduring. The officeholder's judgment may be called into question and usually the general public suspects the officeholder of involvement in the misdeeds. Many otherwise honorable officeholders have seen their political careers destroyed by the failures of their subordinates.

The last failure is actually not a failure so much as it is a natural consequence of humanness. I am referring to the discouragement an officeholder frequently feels.

Any person who has ever held elective office will attest to the frustrations that seem inherent in such positions. The conflicting demands of an intense public, combined with the increasing complexities of the society to which government is called to be the mediator, produce pressures on public officials that tempt them to flee from public service. And this is not a recent malady affecting public servants. It has always been that involvement in the political events of one's time, while exciting and potentially beneficial to the public good, can cause officeholders to yearn for a return to private life.

Way back in 1793, during his service as our nation's first Secretary of State, Thomas Jefferson wrote in a letter to his friend James Madison of his own yearning for a quiet existence far removed from the vicissitudes of public life. Wrote Jefferson: "The motion of my blood no longer keeps time with the tumult of the world. It leads me to seek for happiness in the lap and love of my family, in the society of my neighbors & my books, in the wholesome occupations of my farm & my affairs, in an interest or affection in every bud that opens, in every breath that blows around me, in an entire freedom of rest or motion, of thought or incogitancy, owing account to myself alone of my hours & actions."

These words of Jefferson convey sentiments with which most who have served in public office can identify. When even the best of history's public servants—and certainly Jefferson was among the best of the ages—can grow discouraged and be tempted to throw off the mantle of leadership, it scarcely comes as a surprise that far lesser public officials experience similar emotions!

What do religiously sensitive citizen-politicians do when discouragement comes? They remind themselves that no one ever promised them that life, let alone politics, would be a bed of roses. They pray to the God they worship to give them the twin gifts of patience and persistence. They seek, through the inquiry of God through prayer, and through the inquiry of their minds through introspection, new and better ways of handling their present responsibilities. And they plod on, knowing that the worthiness of their labors are worth the trials of their souls.

Pausing after Sunday morning worship, the author visits with his son, Jeff.

6

Clergy as Citizen-Politicians

The sight of the clergy mixing in politics should not appear unusual. The fact is that an increasing number of the clergy are holding elective office and thousands have become active participants in the discussion and determination of public issues.

A 1977 article in *The Washington Post* begins a chronology of the role of the clergy in politics with a rather dramatic flair: "They came in clerical collars, clutching prayer book or rosary, into the South during the civil rights struggle of the early sixties lending the moral persuasion of the church against bigotry and racism. Then later these ministers and priests and their successors, some fresh from the seminary, marched, prayed in, sat in, were gassed, arrested, clubbed—active participants in the protests against the war in Vietnam."[41]

The author contends that "it is in the last two decades that clergymen in this country have deepened their involvement in politics." He relates that Joseph Rauh, veteran Washington civil rights lawyer, believes testimony by clergy members before a congressional committee provided the needed impetus to gain passage of the 1964 Civil Rights Bill.

The clergy leaders are beginning to realize, in increasing numbers, that running for office is one way of mixing religion and politics. However, for some of the clergy, because of personal characteristics, personalities, and professional status, running for office is not a viable option. Those who do run for office may do so because they are discouraged by the failures of society and disappointed in political efforts to overcome those failures. Along with millions of other Americans, they understand that they, and their parishioners, can become the victims of deficient political practices. They realize the faith they proclaim, the ideals they hold before their flock, and the aspirations they prod their people to seek have become the victims of corrupt politicians who devise and administer corrupt governmental policies. Worse, they see the people they serve become the unfortunate prey of government leaders who betray their constitutional principles.

The clergy are, consequently, usually willing respondents when the appeal is made to mix religion and politics. Although all members of the clergy can and should make a political witness, it is neither advisable nor necessary for all of the clergy to adopt the same format for mixing religion and politics.

I have often said I cannot imagine anything worse than a governmental legislative body composed entirely of pastors. But legislative assemblies without the benefit of a few whose training and vocational choice is that of the professional clergy are bereft of helpful insights that naturally emerge out of a minister's training and experience. The same observation holds true with regard to the activities of political parties, pressure groups, and the governmental bureaucracy. The active involvement by pastors in all spheres of life that affect the political process can be helpful in the attainment of legitimate political goals.

A good example of enlightened and effective political involvement by a clergyman is Missouri's Republican United States Senator, John C. Danforth. An ordained Episcopal minister, Danforth holds both a theological and a law degree from Yale University. Although most of his career has been spent in legal and public service, he has maintained his contact with the church.

During most of his eight years as Attorney General of Missouri, before being elected Senator, Danforth served as Assistant Rector of an Episcopal Church in Jefferson City. He has not hesitated to cast public issues in a moral and ethical light when he deemed it appropriate. Without a doubt he has been a constructive influence in politics and government.

The following discussion may be instructive for the clergy who want to be effective in politics, and encourage lay members of religious institutions to be more receptive to the efforts of ministers to mix religion and politics. Members of some religious bodies are frequently adamant in their insistence that their professional clergy stay away from any involvement with politics and government.

There is an attitude among some non-religious persons, especially among those who consider themselves intellectual sophisticates, that professional religious workers who take stands on political issues are suspect on both intellectual and temperamental grounds. It is as if following a religious vocation makes one unfit for level-headed political participation. Holders of this position seem to feel that the clergy are contaminated with a deadly poison that kills the capacity for reasonable and effective political involvement. Actually, political involvement by the clergy frequently opens up new opportunities for service in the name of God.

Politics as a Field of Ministerial Service

The clergy who become involved in politics find it difficult to escape being called upon to do the work of a minister. I am not referring to the inevitability of pastors being asked to give invocations at political banquets. I am referring to the more personal side of a minister's work, pastoral counseling.

I have been amazed in the sixteen years I have been professionally involved in politics at the number of persons who have come to me for personal counseling. Sometimes it is a question about religion, but just as frequently it is an appeal for help with a very personal problem.

Pastors involved in politics must be very careful how they handle these situations. They will want to be as helpful as possible without causing the individuals to rely on them to the exclusion of utilizing the religious institution of their own faith to minister to their needs on a regular basis. Pastors involved in politics must be particularly careful about performing weddings and officiating at funerals. These are times when individuals need the ministry of their own pastor, and an acquaintance through the individual's political activities should not become a substitute minister image.

Ministers active in politics will be called on to give many public prayers. These are splendid opportunities for the clergy to lead a group of people into a close spiritual relationship with God through offering a meaningful prayer. There are definitely some "don'ts" for prayers offered at political meetings. Among the most important are:

Don't use the prayer to lecture elected officials who are present.
Don't use the prayer to expound personal political views.
Don't use the prayer to display cuteness and cleverness.
Don't pray too long or both God and the audience will wear out.

One problem that faces Christian clergy is whether to use the customary Christian closing. Some members of the Jewish faith are offended with Christian closings in prayers offered before political groups where persons of both Jewish and Christian faiths are present.

A closing I have used on occasion in public groups is meaningful to me and, from the comments of others, has been helpful to them. It goes like this: "We pray in the spirit of him whom some of us believe to be the savior of all humanity and whom all of us recognize as a great and good man. Amen."

One of the marvelous opportunities that ministers involved in politics have is permitting others to know them in a role other than that of a local church pastor. I was amazed, after leaving my parish, at the stereotyped views many lay persons hold of ministers. Ministers do have feet of clay and can be more effective when members of their congregation recognize them as human beings and not as visiting dignitaries from another world. This does not mean that ministers have to pick up all the bad habits of their new associates, but it does suggest they can permit themselves to be human and, in the process, perhaps break down some artificial barriers that exist between the ministry and the people they are called to serve.

Success in political involvement requires ministers to deal with the hard issues of politics. The impediments for effective clergy political involvement are indeed formidable. Any clergyperson who is thinking of entering the political thicket should give these impediments careful scrutiny.

Impediments to Clergy Political Involvement

A major impediment for members of the clergy who want to mix religion and politics is their professional image. Images can be an accurate reflection of a real object or they can be a false rendition. Whether accurate or inaccurate, most persons react, at least initially, to the image in their mind's eye. If that image is negative, according to their values, they may never go to the trouble to ascertain if the reality behind the image is as perceived.

Politicians, with whom the clergy must get involved, generally have a stereotyped image of the clergy as persons concerned with other-worldly affairs, not too knowledgeable about practical matters, and inclined to mouth excessive moralisms. Most politicians conceive ministers to be naive persons who have led sheltered lives and know little about either politics or government. Politicians generally do not think the clergy have any business getting involved in politics because politicians know the seamy side of politics and cannot understand how "persons of God" can allow themselves to get mixed up in such an unholy mess.

Professional politicians may view the clergy in politics with suspicion, resentment, and as a fit target for exploitation.

The minister's loyalty to the party is suspected. Politicians wonder if a pastor can be depended on to stay in the party's boat when the political waters get stormy. The pastor's knowledge of public affairs is a subject of suspicion for most politicians.

While ministering to a congregation in Arkansas in the late fifties, I wrote a letter to United States Senator William F. Fulbright of Arkansas about a speech he had made in the Senate. Part of the text of that letter is as follows: "My main purpose for writing you is to suggest, with the greatest amount of respect for your ability and integrity, something which through the years I have found missing in your utterances in regard to our nation's problems—something which I feel America needs.

"That 'something' is any reference to the spiritual foundations upon which our nation was founded—foundations which give guidance and worth to the education you speak of as being so basic to our way of life. America needs men of your high intellectual and moral caliber who will not only call her back to an intense reliance on education, but who will challenge her to a noble quest for the ultimate meaning of existence.

"We need men like yourself, not to make a 'show' of religious faith, but to point up in a very definite manner the need of America for such faith." I appealed to Senator Fulbright, "for the good of our nation, to let it be known that you realize the basic need America has for such faith and to lend your efforts to those men of goodwill who are striving to bring her to a firm dependence on God."

Fulbright replied promptly, thanking me for the kind words I had written about his speech and then stated his reluctance to deal with spiritual matters. "I do not feel that I am qualified," he wrote, "to deal with the subjects which you and others of your calling are eminently qualified to deal with, and further, the effectiveness of pronouncements on political issues is diminished and subject to misinterpretation, charges of demagoguery and hypocrisy when they are interwoven with spiritual references. In other words, it does not seem to me that political officials should be expected also to be ministers of the gospel. It is quite enough for one man to try to understand and to present in a reasonably concise and clear manner the political issues that confront us in this rather confused era."

The Senator was saying, politely and bluntly, that he would tend to political matters in which he had expertise and that I should stick with spiritual matters. I appreciated his frankness but felt then, as I do now, that a consideration of the spiritual aspects of political questions is worth the trials of enduring charges of demagoguery and hypocrisy.

In my first term in the Missouri legislature I represented a predominantly rural district. Early in the legislative term, a bill was being considered on the regulation of cattle production. Since my county (Saline) was the state's fourth largest producer of cattle and since I had been contacted by some of my farmer constituents about the bill, I rose and spoke on the bill. After I had taken my seat, one of the oldtimers in the legislature walked down the aisle, leaned over and inquired, "What in the hell does a preacher know about cattle? You had better stick to religion."

The minister's image is that of a "pro" in religion, not that of one with credentials qualifying him or her to be astute in any other area. When pastors get out of their field, they will be suspected!

Resentment of the clergy in politics is not uncommon. The presence of pastors cramps the style and language of many persons. They feel uncomfortable with the clergy around and think they cannot be themselves. The facade makes it almost impossible for a minister to deal with such persons on the basis of truth. The pretention that clouds the truth effectively forbids an encounter with the issues as they really are.

Sometimes ministers convey such a "holier-than-thou" attitude that the ensuing resentment is deserved. No one appreciates being looked down upon, and sometimes unconsciously pastors make others think they feel they are superior. The resentment that follows destroys any possibility of the communication needed to deal with political issues in a constructive manner.

Professional members of the clergy are frequently exploited by individual politicians and by political parties. Billy Graham, the evangelist, is thought by many to have been exploited by most of the Presidents during whose terms he has been active as an evangelist. Graham's immense following made him a religious figure with whom politicians of both parties wanted to be seen. Senator Mark Hatfield wrote of this frankly when he voiced concern that Graham's genuine pastoral care for a President might cause him "to overlook how people in the administration could be tempted to exploit that relationship to their own ends."

Exploitation can be the means by which politicians co-opt the religious influence of the clergy or of the religious institution they represent. Ministers who become active in politics must always be on guard so that their public image of standing for the truths of God cannot be plundered by those whose primary aim is to gather greater political power. Since the days when Roman Emperor Constantine co-opted the church for his own political purposes, political parties and personalities have engaged in similar activities.

Pastors involved in politics must be careful not to let their position as ministers be used to advance the political fortunes of an individual or a party. Ministers' positions are held in high esteem by the general public because they are seen as representatives of God. Clever office seekers recognize the influence many ministers have over members of their parish, and frequently are anxious to court their favor for the political help they can provide.

It is perfectly permissible and indeed laudable for ministers, as citizens, to help an individual candidate or to support the party of their choice. But to utilize their roles as ministers, or the structures and activities of the church for political purposes, is always unwise and probably unethical.

Politicians sometimes ask ministers to write letters on church stationery, furnish lists of church members with names and addresses, and may ask ministers to get them invited to speak at church meetings so they can have public exposure. Ministers should politely but firmly refuse all such requests, unless the church is actually seeking such contact. Churches and synagogues should certainly have public forums held there in order to inform members on public issues. But when such forums are held, they ought to be for the purpose of fulfilling the religious institution's spiritual needs and not to advance a particular candidate or a particular political party.

The general public has images of the clergy that are both positive and negative. To some, ministers can do no wrong, and their participation in politics is accepted as indicative of the political wishes of God! Any pastor with that kind of power must be extremely careful about his political activities. Persons holding such views of ministers are ill-advised to elevate the clergy in such a manner.

Sometimes the clergy are so enamored with the American democratic system that it becomes a substitute religion. The nation is always the loser when her religious leaders use their religious influence for the political purpose of promoting idolatry of America. In a real sense, clergymen serve neither the nation nor God when they become so much a part of the political current they cannot be distinguished by their unique religious qualities. Reinhold Niebuhr once observed that "no group within a nation will ever criticise the nation as severely as the nation ought to be criticised, if it does not stand partly outside of the nation." [42]

Ministers' images within the congregations they serve may suffer. Members of the flock are accustomed to hearing their ministers preach, conduct funerals, officiate at weddings, receive persons into the membership of the religious institution, pray in public, and call on the sick and bereaved. They are not accustomed to hearing pastors issue partisan statements, testify at governmental hearings, lambast political opponents, or engage in other overtly political acts.

Nor are the clergy accustomed to political activities by colleagues. Whatever a person's profession, the respect of one's peers is essential to professional stability and self-respect. Political involvement does not usually produce a favorable image of a minister among his peers.

The positive image of the clergy is often a casualty of efforts to become politically involved. This image is not all-important but does occupy a vital spot in human relations. Pastors will do well to consider what kind of an image their political involvement is creating in the mind's eye of politicians, the general public, the members of the religious institution served, and among their peers. They may find they can do little to preserve a legitimate ministerial image but, again, they may find just the opposite. At any rate, the image consequences of political involvement must not be disregarded.

Another impediment for ministers is the inherent divisive nature of politics—as Sidney Hillman phrased it, "the science of how who gets what, when, and why." When groups or persons get things that other groups want, tension and potential divisiveness arise.

In a congregation this divisiveness can lessen a minister's ability to care for the spiritual needs of the members. If the pastor is an avowed, known member of one political party, members of his congregation who are in another political party may experience difficulty in accepting this ministry even in times of severe personal need.

Generally, if ministers take great pains to keep partisan views from their sermons, and absolutely refuse to mix political activities with professional duties, this potential impediment can be overcome. Sometimes just the frank recognition of the potential harm that can be done is sufficient to prevent such divisiveness from doing its mischief.

Another impediment for the clergy is their mobility. Although tenure in pastorates varies from denomination to denomination, most pastors, especially in their early years, make changes frequently. As a consequence, they find it difficult to gain the influence and respect necessary to become effective political leaders.

Of course, they are not alone, for society is increasingly mobile. Few persons live out their lives in the same community in which they were born. In some respects American society is rootless.

For the clergy this means they must strongly emphasize the spiritual aspects of their reasons for involvement in politics. The deeper reasons that prompt the clergy to get involved in politics have a compelling force all their own that may compensate for the diminishing influence that occurs because of impermanence of residence.

A final impediment for clergy involvement in politics is the church-state issue. The clergy is viewed by some as the ultimate defender of the separation of church and state. Others interpret any involvement by pastors in political affairs as an undue encroachment between church and state.

If ministers stay within their own religious tradition in the views they hold and express on church-state relations, they will experience little turmoil. But when they step outside their own religious circle and forcefully pursue political objectives, those who oppose their goals will quickly construct arguments alleging that the pastors are violating the traditional separation of church and state. Ministers who are active in politics, especially when they seek to mix the values of traditional religion with political practices, are certain to experience difficulties.

Most of us prefer neat compartments for our religion and our politics. The mixing of the two is frightful enough, but for a minister to be the catalyst is too much! Separation of church and state has become a sacred American doctrine, and many persons, religious and nonreligious, consider it grossly violated when clergy get involved in politics.

I am not implying that there are not violations of proper church-state relations by the clergy. In a series of rulings over the past quarter of a century, the United States Supreme Court has spelled out rather clearly the guidelines for proper, constitutional relations between church and state. The court has not always been consistent nor accurate in its interpretation of what the Constitution permits. But in the main, it has aided the clergy in understanding the boundaries that must be respected between church and state. Pastors interested in church-state relations and concerned not to overstep these boundaries will find a host of literature available to guide them.

The impediments to ministers in becoming active in politics are substantial but not impossible to overcome. The clergy who are determined not to be shut out of the political realm where vital decisions are made will find ways of moving around these obstacles and becoming bona fide participants in the politics of their time.

Types of Clergy Citizen-Politicians

Any classification scheme is subject to question, but even an incomplete division of clergy into different types of citizen-politicians may be helpful in providing insights on how ministers do go about mixing religion and politics.

Probably the most frequent type is *The Issue Oriented*. Pastors do not, contrary to the limited knowledge of some commentators, live a sheltered life far removed from the hard facts of the cruel world. In their daily work, the clergy come face to face with the problems of poverty, crime, alcoholism, drug abuse, marital discord, child abuse, and ignorance. They see the negative effects of unjust laws and experience firsthand the repercussions of governmental neglect of social problems like poor housing and inadequate public health measures. Parishioners of theirs end up in state prisons, mental hospitals, and other government-administered institutions. When wars come, the clergy serve as chaplains to those doing the fighting and as spiritual advisers to the families waiting anxiously at home for news of their loved ones.

This real world where ministers function among real persons with real problems causes most of them to inquire about the issues which lie beneath the problems with which they have to cope. When pastors realize that a parishioner has a problem because government has failed to act, or has acted improperly or inadequately, they become interested in issues.

Ministers have been in the forefront of many of the critical issue movements of recent years: civil rights, drug abuse, nuclear proliferation, corrections reform, welfare measures, the peace movement. Issues turn pastors on, for they feel they are dealing with substantive matters that affect lives, and they want to become involved in helping the general public face up to issues. Generally, involvement with issues does not automatically usher the clergy into political party participation.

Political parties are made up of persons striving to corner political power for purposes largely determined after the power is won. Most pastors insist on knowing beforehand what issues are going to be addressed by the victorious political power. Therefore, the clergy generally feel more comfortable affiliating themselves with groups that are organized around a single issue. In essence, ministers are more inclined to become political activists through a social pressure group than by means of political party membership.

A second type of clergy citizen-politician is *The Party Gadfly*. These pastors share themselves with all the political parties and most of the issue-oriented groups. They are for all "good things" in the community. Theirs is the shotgun approach to political involvement. They run about blessing many public events and worthwhile causes with their presence. They do not become very deeply involved in any one issue or group because they feel they must save enough of themselves for other issues and groups.

Party gadflies are not useless, but their approach to political involvement makes them almost unknown to any group. Their intentions are undoubtedly the highest, but accomplishments are few.

A third clergy type is *The Party Activist*. These ministers are devout members of an issue group or political party, and do not hesitate to let their activity and loyalty become public knowledge. They attend meetings of their group or party regularly and assume responsibility for their membership.

Party activists frequently become officers of their groups. Some become chaplains of legislative bodies or other governmental groups. Through their active presence they personalize the interests of the religious community, as represented by them, in the party or group.

Sometimes political party activists get so carried away with involvement in their political labors that they lose their religious perspective. Their political involvement becomes their religion. God becomes a Democrat or a Republican and the Chief of whatever issue group commands their loyalty. Such activists need to recall President Lincoln who was not so concerned whether God was on his side but that he was on God's side.

A final type of clergy citizen-politician is *The Officeholder*. For fourteen years I have held public office while maintaining my identity as a clergyman. For over half of those years I held a pastorate in addition to my public service, but since holding a statewide office I have not attempted to carry a full ministerial load. The suggestions which follow are derived largely from my own experiences, but do reflect partially my conversations with and observations of other pastors in public office.

The life of public servants, like that of ministers, is open both to the inspection and the interference of the public. I soon discovered, from a practical standpoint, that my experiences in the ministry with all kinds of people in varying circumstances had furnished a preview of the human involvements that would become mine in public office.

Specifically, I have three observations which may be helpful in evaluating the worth of a minister's serving in public office and what obstacles and opportunities confront a minister in public office.

My first observation is that there are those who question the propriety of ministers serving in elected offices and continuing to serve in the active ministry. Several objections are made, each holding a measure of truth. There are, for instance, all kinds of practical difficulties. Time becomes more precious and more things are left undone in the parish, even with an adequate and cooperative staff. Barriers are erected between the minister-official and those in his congregation of a different political party and/or political philosophy. Then, there is the "image" of the ministry and religious institutions to consider—and we are not speaking of the "public relations" image, but of the deep and abiding image people have of religious institutions and their ministry as representatives of God. An elected official frequently finds himself in situations and places which are not customary habitats for the clergy.

When I first ran for political office my opponent, an incumbent state representative, passed the word around that I would be ineffective as a state representative because as a minister I could not go into the bars and nightclubs where all political decisions are made.

After I was elected, I found my opponent was mistaken on two counts. First, I could go into the bars and nightclubs if it were necessary to do my job. Second, not very many political decisions are made in nightclubs and bars. Actually, more ministers ought to be frequenting bars and nightclubs. They should be there not for the purpose of drinking and reveling, but because people are there who need their help. Frankly, though, I have never found a bar or a nightclub very conducive to effective ministering or politicking or carrying out the governmental business of the people. But if the occasion demands it, a minister involved in politics has to be ready and willing to go wherever it is necessary to do the job.

Of course there are theological difficulties. The matter of separation of church and state can easily become clouded and made tragically indistinct. Just as it is disastrous whenever the religious institutions come under the control of the state, it is just as unfortunate whenever—however subtle it is—the state becomes the slave of an ecclesiastical body.

Yet, in spite of these difficulties, there is a need for ministers to serve in public offices. Ministers, with their background of training in theology and ethics and with their intimate acquaintance with the deep foundations of life, belong in those bodies which make our laws. They can bring viewpoints to legislative considerations that need representation and which are extremely valuable in structuring a society which has moral depth as well as economic and political stability.

A second observation is that ideals and principles, as important as they are, are not sufficient ingredients to guarantee that we shall have just laws and good government. The ministry, and some dedicated church leaders, are apt to overplay the importance of these and consequently incur the opposition of other officials to their inclusion in the processes of government. Professional public servants of demonstrated ability have been known, rightly or wrongly, to get the impression that religious bodies advance views that are highly idealistic but extremely unrealistic and impractical. Sometimes the charge is made, and possibly with some justification, that religious bodies are too willing to speak on any and all subjects without first gathering the facts.

Therefore, clergy officeholders must be not only idealistic and dedicated to high principles, but must be competent. It is well to speak out concerning convictions, but to speak out in ignorance or against a background of unfamiliarity with the situation is most unwise.

Further, a pastor in public office must possess an open mind. The clergy are so accustomed to letting people and the world know in well oiled and flowery terms what is wrong with everything that they are tempted to continue in this role as officeholders. Very often everything is not what it seems at first glance, and the better part of wisdom is to wait a while before jumping to conclusions which may later rise up to haunt one. Henry David Thoreau once observed that there are some ministers who spoke of God "as if they enjoyed a monopoly of the subject" and "who could not bear [to hear] all kinds of opinions."[43] Unfortunately this same observation is too often true of rank and file ministers. They seem to feel, or at least leave the impression, that they have all knowledge on all questions because they seek to speak in the name of God. How foolish the clergy is not to recognize that sometimes their members do not mirror God to the world as he actually is. A little humility is never out of character.

If ministers are to be effective in bringing influence to bear in government, they must not underestimate how difficult it is in a democracy for public officials to pursue what they think is right.

As officeholders, ministers must be willing to provide ethical and moral leadership, even if such leadership costs them their elected positions. There is a modern tendency to glorify the past, bemoan the present, and insist the country does not turn out the quality of leaders it did in days gone by. Courageous ministers in public office can do much to disprove contentions that moral leadership is a thing of the past.

The clergy must not sell short the importance of conveying to their colleagues in public office their moral and ethical concerns about issues under consideration. It is not the business of government to be the custodian of morals nor the repository of ethics; but it is the business of government to conduct its affairs in a moral and ethical manner. It is self-evident, America's forefathers claimed, that people are to be governed morally and ethically in this land. If ministers in office cannot be depended upon to proclaim this truth, from whom will it be heard?

Pastors trying to be officeholders soon discover that concern for stable government requires involvement in the political life of America. Familiarity with the dynamics of politics and the adaptation of them to worthy ends becomes a major task. To shut oneself off from the world of politics, calling it "dirty" and beneath the "dignity" of religion, is foolish. Politics is much too fundamental in structuring our way of life to be left to those who would serve only selfish ends. But it is foolish for clergy to become officeholders under the illusion that their service will be continually exciting and will not exact changes in their lives. Politics is not pleasant at times. Values are challenged more frequently in the political world than they are in the pastorate.

It is a common teaching among theologians that pride is the greatest sin of all. Ministers in public office have to be constantly on guard lest they become victims of deadly pride. Everyone expects ministers to be for honesty, justice, virtue. Unfortunately, they may forget that persons are not automatically honest, or just or virtuous. Ministers are human, too, and must work at these ideals.

The clergy in politics are expected to live up to their values. They are, so to speak, "under the gun." The floodlights of public opinion are upon them and any deviation from the highest values are noted quickly.

The frustration for ministers in politics is that even as they try to live up to these values, they will be accused or perceived by political opponents of being overly pious. The response of ministers must be *first* to make certain they are not pious frauds and *second* not to let such accusations prod them into unpious acts to prove they are not pious!

There is a legitimate place in politics for the full time involvement of clergy. Obviously not all clergy should seek such involvement, but those who feel they can best serve God in public office should not hesitate to accept the challenge.

People frequently ask if there is a significant political advantage for ministers involved in politics. Their assumption is that ministers running for office will garner more votes because of their vocation. My experience has been that the advantages are well-balanced by some significant disadvantages. It is true that the ministry, as a profession, enjoys a higher level of trust from the general public than does the vocation of politician. However, there exists in many minds a firm feeling that ministers do not belong in politics, and probably as many feel that way as do those who are encouraged to vote for candidates because they are ministers. I have always felt it important not to hide the fact that I am a minister, nor to make an issue of the fact that I am.

Whether as officeholders or in some other capacity, the clergy are needed as active participants in the political world. Along with the witness of others, their presence can often be the added ingredient that turns a foul broth into a delightful appetizer. Whether the meal that follows will satisfy depends on other ingredients in the political world.

7

Amen!

Years ago, especially in rural churches, it was customary to "Amen" a preacher when someone in the congregation agreed with what the minister was saying. Since the literal meaning of "Amen" is "truly" or "verily," the loud "Amen" meant that the person felt that what was being said was true. This was a way of expressing public confidence in the message being preached. Although not many congregations continue the practice of spontaneous Amens, most prayers are concluded with "Amen" and in that context it has come to mean "so be it."

"Amen" seems to be a fitting word to ascribe to the concluding pages of a book that issues a call to action. My hope is that persons reading these words will agree that the mixing of religion and politics ought to come to pass—Amen, so be it! If God does, in fact, care about politicians; if he smiles upon those who become involved in politics in order to bring into existence a public policy in accord with God's purposes, why should any religiously sensitive citizen-politician hesitate to mix the two?

The failure to mix religion and politics is widespread. Many of our citizens, among whom are a considerable number of religiously sensitive persons, do not believe politics and the politicians it spawns, are worthy of their time, talents, or money. In vast numbers, Americans refuse to come forth with a loud "Amen" to suggestions that they actively mix religion and politics.

This situation shouldn't be permitted to continue. Religion and politics have too much in common to be kept apart. But both fields are complex and potentially devastating to any who explore their depths and are serious about their practical implications for their own lives and times. Therefore, religiously sensitive citizen-politicians should be cautious but obvious as they mix religion and politics.

Why Persons Refuse to Mix Religion and Politics

No claim is made that the following seven reasons for refusing to mix religion and politics are all-inclusive. Nor does every person who refuses to mix religion and politics base that refusal on all seven reasons.

But many persons who accept the veracity of these statements cling to them tenaciously as logical explanations for their antagonism toward mixing religion and politics.

Reason No. 1 When you mix religion and politics, conflict emerges that divides persons into religious camps and results in ill-feelings.

A common reaction to efforts to mix religion and politics can be phrased: "When you mix religion and politics, you may cause Protestants to fight Catholics, Christians to fight Jews, or all religiously oriented persons to be in opposition to everyone else. The result is a divided community."

Such a reaction is accurate if persons are limited by their own negativism. But those who look beneath the surface of the obvious tensions—when politics must justify its positions and religion must demonstrate its relevance—are aware that the resultant conflict is both inevitable and often desirable.

I remember as a child, asking my mother what it was like to have a baby—didn't it hurt? I'll never forget her reply, "Yes, of course, but once you have your baby in your arms you forget all about the pain and are at peace."

So it is with the conflict between religion and politics. If moral policies and relevant religion are to be born into society, there will be first travail and pain, but frequently this discomfort ushers in an era of peace and calm.

Americans alternately are repulsed and refreshed by instances of conflict among groups, institutions, and ideological forces within our nation. In its more rational moments, the nation recognizes the inevitability of contrasting views colliding when each seeks public acceptance and approval.

But the United States does not always act on the basis of rational considerations. Especially in religious matters and political procedures people are inclined to be guided more by their emotions than by their minds. As a consequence, whenever religious and political positions conflict, there is often more heat than light.

Religiously sensitive persons who accept the challenge to mix religion and politics can expect to experience more situations of intense conflict. When the political stakes are high and the religious feelings run deep, only the more naive expect the combination of the two to result in a Pollyanna type encounter where everyone agrees that everything is wonderful.

In a society as pluralistic as America, avoidance of conflict is impossible. We Americans differ economically, ethically, religiously, racially, culturally, and in age. The geographical localities where we reside provide us with a range of interests that tend to make the desires of persons in one section of the country different from the desires of persons living in other sections of the country. Actually, the reason politics is necessary is to mediate inevitable conflict. The political process is the means used in a democracy to prevent conflict-producing situations from getting out of hand and causing a continual state of anarchy.

Any realistic view of politics takes into account the fact that people do disagree, frequently because they are uninformed. They are like the persons whose voices become louder as it becomes obvious they do not know what they are saying. People tend to be emotional and even irrational when discussing either religion or politics. Such conflict just cannot be avoided in a true democracy. Nor should conflict be stifled. To bottle up the deep concerns of persons beneath the surface of society causes them to fester and eventually contaminate the very foundations of society.

Religiously sensitive persons are aware that Americans are divided into ideological camps. To deny the existence of such divisions in our society is both inaccurate and unwise. Conflicting groups can never work out their differences if the very existence of their differences is not admitted. The distrust and suspicion which persons hold toward people and groups different from themselves can never be overcome by erecting barriers for keeping separate contrasting viewpoints, organizations, and institutions.

A case in point is the fetish in America of the concept of the separation of church and state. Sometimes I wish Jefferson had never written about the wall of separation between church and state because walls and fences do not make good neighbors. Persons who know the boundary lines of their own property do not need a fence or wall to remind them where their property leaves off and their neighbor's begins. The erection of walls makes communication between neighbors more difficult. When neighbors fail to communicate, each suspects what is going on behind the wall separating the two.

In America, segments of the religious community are so suspicious of other religious groups that they overlook trends in our society that are much more damaging to the future of our country than the remote possibility of the emerging of a monolithic religious group gaining political control of the country.

I was raised in a rather strong Protestant family. I can recall fears expressed of the monolithic invincibility of the Roman Catholic Church. The Roman Catholic Church was pictured as a superhuman institution that would live forever and ultimately work its political and spiritual will upon the entire world. I have long since disposed of any such foolish notions and recognize that this great religious body is the ally, and not the enemy, of those who are concerned that God's will become the guiding light for our corporate and individual ways. Obviously the Roman Catholic Church takes positions on various public issues at variance with positions taken by other religious bodies. On the other hand, there has been and will continue to be, within the Roman Catholic Church, division of opinion on issues, just as there is division of opinion on specific issues among members of other religious bodies.

The pluralism of our society is more widespread than is commonly recognized. Religious groups are difficult to divide into camps on the basis of their religious attitudes toward public issues. Agreement among the members of the same religious bodies is not as widespread as is commonly supposed.

Put it down as certain: conflict will be encountered in the political arena. The role of the religious person is to emphasize the religious and ethical dimensions of issues with which the body politic must concern itself. The failure to recognize public issues as being representative of basically religious and ethical concerns prevents these issues from being dealt with in the most effective manner. This does not mean that a religious interpretation or meaning should be read into a political issue when the religious or ethical aspect is not fundamental. However, the continual disregard of religious and ethical questions that arise naturally in the consideration of many public issues results in their never being effectively resolved.

To refuse to give a loud "Amen" to the mixing of religion and politics because of fear that persons will be divided into religious camps and ill feelings will result is a flimsy excuse at best. Conflict is both inevitable and highly desirable. In the American political process the way conflicts are met is through compromise, which raises another reason which must be resolved.

Reason No. 2 Politics requires compromise, and a truly religious person cannot compromise.

The aversion to compromise of any sort is deeply embedded in the consciousness of most religious persons. Persons do not take lightly any belief to which they ascribe a religious meaning. Because they are serious about their religion, the slightest implication that their religious views are open to question is greeted with scorn. Religious literature, the environment in which religious persons live, the religious institutions to which they belong, and the associates who share their religious experiences all unite to program religious persons to reject the merest suggestion of compromise. I recently read a prayer by the English Anglican writer, William Barclay, which illustrates clearly the disrepute in which compromise is held among some religious persons. The prayer goes like this: "Grant unto us the loyalty which will be true to Thee, even though all men deny Thee, and which will never stoop to compromise.

"Grant unto us the purity which can resist all the seductions of temptation, and which can never be turned from the straight way."[44]

Religious people are consistently exposed to this kind of all-or-nothing-at-all philosophy conveyed by Barclay's prayer. In their worship services, in their conversations, in the sermons they hear, in the sacred books they read, and in many other experiences, they are reminded that people who are truly religious just do not compromise *at all.*

This kind of an attitude fosters a mentality which actually believes it is possible to see life in black and white. Religious people are convinced that some things are right and some things are wrong and that it is easy to distinguish between the two. They believe those who cannot distinguish between the two probably lack moral sensitivity.

President Jimmy Carter evaluates himself as the kind of person who, as he puts it, does not "know how to compromise on any principle I believe is right." Carter goes on to observe that "Unthinking noncompromise is of course foolish; but maybe this is a time, on matters of principle, for an absence of compromise."[45] Religious persons claim there is never a time for compromise on principle and insist on the right to define the principles.

This rigid position would be acceptable if every religious person had a personal pipeline to God. Unfortunately, equally sincere and devout persons can disagree sharply on God's will in given circumstances.

The case for compromise rests on man's fallibility. Human views of current events do not become divine commentaries just because they are delivered by religious persons. Nor can restrictions be placed by persons on how, where, when, or through what medium God will convey his purposes to mankind. Therefore, religiously sensitive persons are well advised to exercise caution in claiming their positions are not open to compromise. The refusal to compromise may be the very act whereby God's will is denied entrance into human affairs.

How true it is that compromises are made almost every day by almost everybody. What is possible is always a valid consideration. To accept the fruits of a compromise, damaged though they be, is infinitely better than to get no fruit at all. And that frequently is the only choice available in a political situation.

When difficulties emerge in the public arena that require careful compromise, the religious person who possesses a sense of people's temporalness is fortunate. Divine solutions to human problems are not within the realm of possibility for a human being to invoke. People must be content with human responses which, hopefully, are aided by their faith in God. A truly religious person will compromise many times simply because there is no other way whereby any progress can be made toward the attainment of the goals of religion.

Many religious persons refuse to compromise because of a naive conviction that to refuse to compromise is to remain pure. Maybe they are right for, in a sense, no one who engages in politics remains pure. The easiest route to travel may be the rigid path of no compromise at all. That way, issues really do not have to be thought through. Surface responses can be made to issues that actually go to the very heart of the hard realities of contemporary life. Purity can be maintained outwardly, and the accolades of the world will be given for willingness to stand by principle. But the cost of unyielding adherence to a principle which is claimed as the truth of God may be to fail to resolve a critical issue which is tearing away the very fabric of a decent life for God's people.

I sometimes think the word "settlement" ought to be substituted for "compromise," for a compromise is really a settlement between competing parties. Both sides have to give a little in order to come to an agreement by which both can live in peace.

Compromise is not always an easy goal to achieve, nor are some of the political compromises always pleasing to the tastes and likes of politicians. But in a democracy, the will of the majority prevails and thus some cannot have their own way. Those who lack the temperamental capacity to compromise, to enter into settlements, will be uncomfortable in politics at any level.

In 1967-68 I served as chairman of a commission charged with the responsibility of devising a master plan for the reorganization of Missouri's more than 800 local school districts. The nine members of the commission were divided on whether to recommend what it considered an ideal plan of state school district organization or a more modest plan that would be better than what the state had, but far from the ideal. Finally, the commission recommended the ideal, and it was soundly rejected by both the state legislature and the general public. Had the commission been content to propose a less radical plan, I believe most recommendations would have been accepted, and today Missouri's school district structure and quality of education would be better than it is. By holding out for the ideal, little was achieved, and even the opportunity to continue to labor for the ideal was set back for years.

Truly religious persons must accept the fact that they reside in an imperfect world that will not respond to perfect solutions. They must also accept the fact that the possibility of their devising a perfect solution is impossible! Reinhold Niebuhr's observation that "the realisation of the pure ideal in history is indeed expected, but it is really too pure to have any possibility of complete realisation,"[46] ought to be a warning against expecting divine answers from human solutions.

To witness effectively in the world of politics, religious persons have to have the flexibility to compromise again and again. Although there are limits to compromise, those limits will rise naturally in the conscience of religious people. When their consciences, guided by faith and wisdom, say "stop compromising," it is time to stop compromising. Until that time, compromise is a means we can utilize to aid in mixing religion and politics.

Reason No. 3 The injection of religious considerations into the political process diverts persons from resolving critical political issues.

Religion has always had a way of grasping people and holding them tightly once it gets their attention. The fear that preoccupation with religion will lead to neglect of political duties is solidly founded on the basis of historical occurrences. Many German Christians felt their neglect of political participation permitted the rise of Hitler and his methodical elimination of German Jews.

Religion is concerned with eternal principles and the human procedures that logically evolve from a reliance on these principles. When people cannot agree on either the principles or how to apply them, and spend precious time in debating either or both, it can become disconcerting to those who are aware of critical problems being left untended while the debate rages.

Religion is viewed by many as a forum for talk. The idea of action resulting from such talk is foreign to their thinking. Unfortunately, these views of the impotence of religion are valid more often than religious people like to admit. The history of nearly all faiths is filled with instances too numerous to relate of endless debate over minute points while the needs of society were neglected. Religious Neros have often fiddled while their Romes burned.

If political issues are resolved without due consideration of their religious and ethical implications, the consequences can be just as damaging. There are some political issues, such as abortion, equal rights for women and minorities, capital punishment, church-state relations and child abuse, which have obvious religious and ethical overtones. There are other issues, such as the development of a housing policy, regulation of banks, or the building of roads and highways, where the religious and ethical implications are not so apparent, but they are there. A housing policy that discriminates against the poor and minorities obviously becomes a religious and ethical issue as do banking laws that permit advantage to be taken of consumers unaccustomed to dealing in the world of finance. Super highways that are routed around the homes of the wealthy but which are laid straight through a neighborhood of modest but proud homeowners raise questions about the fairness of government policies.

Religiously sensitive citizen-politicians can help keep their religiously-oriented comrades on target. They can insist that purely religious issues be confined within the walls of religious groups. Just as strongly, they can insist that the religious and ethical implications of public issues be given due consideration.

Among many in this nation there is an attitude that parades itself as "intellectual sophistication" that refuses to accept the claims of religion on political issues. Those who are adverse to accepting the input of religion are on shaky historical grounds. As newspaperman David Kucharsky notes, "This idea flies in the face of our whole past because much present law in the democratic countries of the world is rooted in Judeo-Christian teaching."[47] Kucharsky does not believe there ever has been a cut-off date for the influence of religion in politics. He advises people who suggest religious dogma must not be injected into national policy or political strategy to think a little harder because all have sets of religious beliefs (secularistic or spiritual) from which they act, whether or not they realize it.

On the other hand, there are purely private concerns of a religious nature that must be protected from the intrusion of government. That is what the First Amendment to the Constitution is all about. "Congress shall make no law respecting an establishment of religion, or prohibiting the free exercise thereof." There are times when every individual has the right, when exercising his religious faith, to refuse admittance to either government or politics.

Reason No. 4 In a democracy, religion should not be brought into political deliberations because many persons do not have any religious convictions.

Those who hew to this line of reasoning usually go on to warn against forcing citizens in a democracy to consider religious issues when they have no interest in religion. This school of thought contends that the First Amendment was designed to protect citizens from violation of their right to be religious or not.

To force religion on anyone is not only contrary to American constitutional principles but contrary to the teachings of most religions. True religion is a matter of faith freely given. If belief is a response to fear or force, the basis for belief is gone once the fear is gone or the force removed.

The simple truth is that what some call religion others call something else: determination, goodness, love, virtue, peace, etc. The key to understanding people and getting along with them without sacrificing basic religious convictions is the ability to translate what others say into what they mean.

Henry David Thoreau wrote that "if a man does not keep pace with his companions, perhaps it is because he hears a different drummer." Only the foolish and egotistical insist that their hearing is so perfect that only they hear the drums of God. Others may travel a different path and still arrive at the same destination.

Every society must develop a social consensus. Laws cannot be effective until there is a consensus on what society agrees is of universal value. Those moral assumptions, shared convictions, or common values are religion to some and philosophy to others. To address them in public life and to elevate their importance in politics is not to force them on anyone. Rather, acknowledgment of their worth is a means of striving for agreement on a set of values by which people can live together in peace.

In President Jimmy Carter's book, *Why Not the Best?* his contention is that "there is no legitimate reason why government should not represent the highest possible common ideals and characteristics of the people who form and support it." [48] Most would quickly agree that Carter's aspirations are worthy, but a large number of the people would probably also agree that most governments do not reflect the highest ideals of the people.

If these high aspirations are to become reflective of government, those who hold them must be willing to become active in politics and government. Not by words alone, but also by deeds do aspirations become a part of the flesh and blood of the body politic. If faithfulness to values is perceived as a veiled attempt to foist religion on unwilling subjects, the religiously sensitive citizen-politician has no choice but to continue being faithful. Religious persons have just as much right to practice their religion as persons who consider themselves non-religious have the right to practice what they consider to be a religiousless life!

Reason No. 5 I'm not interested in either religion or politics.

Apathetic and lazy people have minds of children. They refuse to say "Amen" to mixing religion and politics simply because they do not want to be bothered with either. Their lives are busy without the added burden of figuring out what they believe or trying to be a factor in the determination of public policies. Career requirements, family activities, and the pursuit of material and sensual happiness leave them little time to develop either a sentiment or a receptivity to religion or politics.

The world is full of people who do not, to use their blunt language, give a damn about politics. Their attitude toward politics, when they think about it (which is seldom), oscillates between apathy and resentment. They do not see the connection between their personal disregard of politics and the emergence of public policies which they personally abhor. Their answer to the disintegration of public life is to complain and blame the politicians for getting the country into such a mess. They never have grasped the concept of democracy as a government controlled by people who care and who give expression to their caring through active participation in politics.

In the summer of 1976, the Bicentennial of the United States, the noted American columnist Peter Lisagor was dying of cancer. Shortly before he died, he wrote a column published on July 3, 1976, in which he observed that "American society has shown itself to be durable, but," he wrote, "its needs cannot be left untended." Then he concluded with this very pointed observation that preaches its own sermon to the politically apathetic: "Democracy, such as it is, can survive almost anything but the neglect of its people, or their indifference." [49]

Commitment and participation in activities as unrewarding as politics are laughable to persons who are wrapped up in themselves. So how can the politically apathetic be jolted out of their indifference? There is no certain method, but there are many possible remedies. An effort has been made here to underline the importance of politics so that readers might question any reticence they have to become politically involved. Political parties, civic groups, columnists and commentators, educational institutions, and a multitude of other persons and groups use a variety of ways to shake Americans out of their apathy. Disinterest in politics is a critical problem for us.

Unfortunately, apathy toward politics is frequently extensive among deeply religious persons. The religious who neglect politics may be so enamored with the importance of faith in God and the doctrines developed by the religious body to which they belong that nothing else matters. The idea that God works through people and the political organizations we have developed is foreign to their thinking. They tolerate politics and politicians but attach little value to the political process and the politicians.

It is not difficult to understand that some politically apathetic persons may also be apathetic toward religion. Both organized religion and organized politics require a breadth of vision and a degree of selflessness that is seldom characteristic of those who disdain active participation in organizations. What is more difficult to perceive is the disregard of religion by many political activists.

The political elite usually do not manifest much interest in religious matters. They have no patience with religious "talk" and, if they had their way, would forever banish such discussion. They distrust the emotional potential of religion. Usually the unspoken but very real fear of the political activist is that the power unleashed when persons follow their religious feelings is emotional and mindless and seldom constructive.

I can emphathize with this attitude. Few experiences are more frightening than confrontation and opposition by persons who are convinced that their cause has the personal blessing of God. In the name of religion, rattlesnakes are handled, persons have been burned at the stake, and holy wars have been fought.

An excellent illustration of this fear is expressed in the following letter from a reader to the editor of *The New York Times:* "There is a very basic reason why many people distrust an officeholder who has strong religious convictions. There is a concern that the officeholder who is convinced he is doing the right thing because his decisions are God-inspired through prayer may brook no challenge. Who can argue with the self-righteous leader who believes he is listening to and obeying the true word of God?" Admittedly, such a convinced believer could create chaos. History records many unfortunate deeds of those who were confident they were doing God's will on earth. Among the most recent are the tragic suicides of nearly one thousand persons in a religious orgy at Jonestown, Guyana, in late 1978.

Those who proclaim no interest in either politics or religion are to be pitied. They are turning away from two areas of life that are both essential and exciting. Their refusal to say "Amen" to the mixing of religion and politics because of their rejection of both reveals the poverty of their lives.

Reason No. 6 Politicians are not very respectable people and if I get involved in politics I may turn out to be just another politician.

Open war seems to have been declared on politicians in the United States. In recent years candidates able to convince voters they are *not* politicians have the best chance of being elected.

I recall being introduced to a group of people at a ground-breaking ceremony for a housing complex for the elderly in a small Missouri city with these words: "Our speaker today is a man of God and a servant of the people. He is not a politician." My inclination was to respond that I am a politician because I want to serve the people and be faithful to God. I am convinced that there are thousands of officeholders throughout this nation who are politicians because they, too, view public service as a worthy means of serving God and others.

The number of Americans who believe political service can be a means of serving God is rapidly diminishing. The average American not only distrusts politicians but doubts if God, who loves even the disreputable sinner, will have anything to do with politicians.

In June 1978, Proposition 13, the Jarvis-Gann tax-cutting amendment to California's state constitution, passed by a tremendous margin. Its passage was widely heralded throughout the nation as a taxpayer's revolt. Others, like Lee Branstool, a stockbroker from San Mateo, California, described the vote as "a groundswell against the politicians. This was an opportunity to kind of sock it to 'em."

Even those who have labored in the political vineyard want to sock it to politicians because they doubt the value of politics. William E. Simon, after four years' service as a cabinet member under Presidents Nixon and Ford, concluded, "the *last* thing to do is to fight conventionally in the political arena, . . ."[50] if blows are to be struck for political sanity in American life. Simon admits he is partisan enough to wish to see members of his party hold office, but has learned that it solves nothing fundamental. With these sentiments many Americans agree but wish they did not. The yearning for a political system in which political efforts do meet with success is pervasive. Americans want to believe political speeches that promise that results will be forthcoming if they will get actively involved in politics.

Actually, even people like Secretary Simon do not heed their own advice. As a member of the federal government and since, Simon has been active in politics. And, later in the same book where he states political participation solves nothing, he contradicts himself by writing: "Get involved in politics—in campaigns from the town council to the White House . . . . Run yourself. Government is far too important to be left to the professional politicians, the wet-finger-in-the-wind types whose purposes are uncontaminated by principles." [51]

Any democratic society that continually degrades and belittles its political leaders is sowing seeds of anarchy. The expression of dissatisfaction and harsh criticism is not only valid but essential to the decision-making process in a democracy. But when these negative observations feed on themselves and never result in positive actions to correct the cause of the dissatisfaction, a tidal wave of criticism may inundate a governmental system and cause its fall.

Politics can become utterly disgusting. To permit every kook in the land to have a say can become a test of patience. To insist on complete exposure for all governmental actions does result in public knowledge of a multitude of disturbing government practices that cause the public's respect for government and politicians to be lessened. No wonder people lose confidence in the capacity of democratic governments to govern effectively.

What people do not realize is that the way democracy does govern is by permitting all views, however kooky they are, to be expressed. Only when all the alternatives are exposed can free people make free choices through their freely elected representatives.

In the thirties German citizens had "enough" of politics and turned their political problems over to Hitler. It can happen here if the nation's rising disaffection with politics is not matched by rising participation in politics by caring persons.

Reason No. 7 I have too much to do to be successful in my own work and, besides, we've got too much government already.

Many refuse to participate in politics simply because they are busy looking out for themselves. As a common saying puts it, "If you don't look out for number one, no one else will." Greed is the inevitable consequence of such a philosophy of life. Greed may be used for constructive purposes, but as an underlying theme, greed provides a very discordant background for any life.

It is so easy for preoccupation with the realities of certain negative aspects of human nature, like greed, to blind the mind and the spirit to the positive possibilities of persons. These positive possibilities never surface for some because preoccupation with the negative leaves no energy or time to accentuate the positive.

A case in point is the legitimate concern of many Americans about the increasing involvement of government in nearly every area of society. This governmental involvement is viewed as negative because of the resulting restriction on human freedom and the increase in taxes necessary to finance the rising costs of government. Add to this the childish desire of people to have all that is wanted right now and pay for it tomorrow—the result is an escalating national debt.

The response of many to this state of affairs is to react negatively to government and the politics that determine who will run government. The culprits are the politicians. Do away with them and, so it appears, the problems will be solved.

But is the answer so simple?

Contrary to such appealing arguments, the underlying danger to freedoms we hold dear, is not the deeds of politicians. Nor is it the nation's propensity to expand the central role of government in all areas of life. The gradual assumption by government of social, economic, and even quasi-religious responsibilities is a fact of our nation's history since the beginning of this century. William Simon is right when he contends that "the incessant spawning and modification of laws, regulations, programs, and 'national purposes' are the expressions of a state which sees its primary function as a controller of citizens."

To get at the real danger to our freedoms, we need to look beneath these outward evidences of unwholesome changes. What we find is steady erosion of concern by American people with spiritual values that emerge out of the love of God as expressed by one person in dealing with another person. Our people are obsessed with money and the things money can buy. Naked materialism stalks the land; greed for things, for sex, for drugs, for power has become the motivating force in too many lives.

But, beneath the surface, Americans are dimly aware that the gratification of their insatiable greed does not satisfy their hunger for the true satisfactions that come from pursuing the traditional values based on service to others.

The American emphasis on personal incentive and its essentiality to the American free enterprise system is valid but must not be permitted to be a substitute for God. Too many Americans worship at the shrine of the capitalistic market. They see all human and social and economic problems being solved once parasitic government is banished to the fringes of life.

But is the excessiveness of government to be exchanged for the excessiveness of market-worshipping legions of people? Is not the deeper need for a recognition that people—whether the president of a corporation or the President of the United States; whether a factory worker or a white collar worker; whether a farm hand or the owner of 1,000 acres of prime land . . . people are people? As such, they are subject to the frailties and virtues of the human flesh but are also the locus of the human spirit which is capable of responding to the Divine Presence.

The turning back of greed is a constant struggle. It does not help for economic leaders to disregard the stark reality of greed's constant presence. I concur that America's free enterprise system encourages maximum productivity by emphasizing our competitive instinct and our innate desire to excel and reap rewards for our efforts. I agree that America's democratic governments encourage wide participation in politics by fashioning a system which provides gratification for those competitive drives in our ceaseless quest for personal possession of power.

But both a free enterprise economy and a democratic governmental system invite trouble of mammoth proportions by disregarding or glossing over our divine origin.

Laudable goals for citizens cannot be achieved if the very nature of persons as creatures of God is not in the forefront of the economic and political discussions that precede the making and execution of political decisions.

Human beings, as they seek to make decisions, are politicians. Their efforts are to evolve policies with which the majority can agree. Their labors are needed and are worthy.

Therefore it always hurts when people, who ought to know better, mouth sayings about politicians that reveal both their cynicism and lack of appreciation for the difficult task of working out public policies in a diverse land like ours. How often I hear people say of politicians, "If you've met one, you've met them all. They're all alike!" Or, "That's a politician for you!" Or, "He talks like a politician."

No wonder the young people of our nation so often turn from consideration of politics as a vocational alternative. Until genuine respect is regained for politicians, the number who say "Amen" to mixing politics and religion is unlikely to increase.

When citizens insist on leaving religion on the fringes of politics, the consequent absence of spiritual discussions effectively results in decisions without a spiritual base.

The harm done by excluding religion from politics causes many new problems and contributes to the nation's inability to solve others. I am convinced that religiously sensitive persons must become conscientious citizen-politicians if there are to be satisfactory and effective solutions to the public policy problems that confront every generation. The major difference between the political problems of today and those of other times in history is that today's citizens are responsible for making today's decisions.

During World War II a German pastor named Dietrich Bonhoeffer was imprisoned and eventually put to death by the Nazis. His spiritual insights take on special meaning because of the atmosphere of persecution which surrounded his final years. Bonhoeffer wrote that for human beings, God "must be found at the centre of life: in life, and not only in death; in health and vigor, and not only in suffering; in activity, and not only in sin." Religion cannot be relegated to a compartment of life and separated from other activities. Right in the midst of political activity religiously sensitive persons should be found, bearing witness to what they believe is God's will for them as persons and for the political order in which they participate.

It does not matter to such persons that their efforts may be unsuccessful. They only know that something within implores them to reach for the unreachable, to dream the impossible and then try to attain it!

It ultimately does not matter what the political results are. The destiny of the world is not in our hands, but in God's. Persons will make whatever contribution they can and then, when their time comes to move on, they'll leave the stage of life so the spotlight may focus on those who are yet to make their appearance. While religiously sensitive persons have the stage, in this instance the political stage, they must act. They must be a mixer of religion and politics, satisfied that God really does care about politicians too!

We Americans must not turn our backs on the call to mix religion and politics. The temptation is great to do so; the way of politics is difficult, and the worldly rewards are few. But the good that can be done by even one lone religious politician is immeasurable. Efforts of individual politicians to mix religion and politics may appear as only a drop in the bucket, but those drops are important!

EPILOGUE

Why I Am Involved in Politics

It occurs to me that anyone who has the persistence to read to the end of this book or who is clever enough to turn to the closing pages for a taste before deciding whether to undertake the whole book, deserves a frank, unembellished statement about why I am involved in politics.

One way of explaining why something is done is to begin by listing all the invalid reasons.

I am not in politics because of disenchantment with organized religion. It would be natural to hold such suspicions of a clergyman who has exchanged his clerical gown for the running togs of a politician. But in this case that is not true.

Actually, I never intended to leave the pastorate and may someday return. In the interim, I remain convinced that the organized expression of religious faith is absolutely essential.

There was a time when I joined the ranks of those accusing religious institutions of moral hypocrisy. I felt some kinship with the social revolutionaries of the sixties who challenged America's traditional way of life and proclaimed corruption to be pervasive in society's institutions.

Americans, during that era, were dismayed that institutions had failed them to some degree. An emphasis on materialism caused some people to believe that religion was irrelevant and even an obstruction to happiness. For a time, our religious institutions did not respond adequately to that challenge.

So the church, whether of Roman or Protestant persuasion, came under fire in such writings as Harvey Cox's *The Secular City*, Fredrick Keller Stamm's *If This Be Religion*, and Paul Tillich's *The Shaking of the Foundations*. In the Jewish community, the influence of rabbis and the institutions they served was questioned.

It was not long until the statistic readers noticed that the upsurge of church attendance and participation that followed the close of World War II had subsided.

The demise of the religious institutions was really the outward evidence of a contemporary flight from religion. A collective faith-gap threatened to topple religion itself from its previously dominant role in influencing the course of human lives and society itself.

An increasing number of persons felt they had outgrown their need for religion. Many maintained, and some still do, that personal morality and social ethics are important but that religion is passé, irrelevant, and possibly even an obstruction to human happiness and social development.

The role of religion, according to conventional perception, was relegated to that of pure pomp, and consequently in this passing era there was rebellion against the church and synagogue.

The organization—the establishment—the system: these were the enemies in the sixties.

Thankfully, that era has passed and America has survived. It survived because responsible leaders corrected many of the shortcomings of impcrtant institutions and showed that they are relevant to life.

It is not possible to live without established institutions. It is not possible to live without participation in them. I have learned that it is foolish to destroy the religious roots that are the source of religious institutions.

The turbulent sixties proved that American institutions, especially her religious institutions, must be preserved by responsible citizens. There is no other way to maintain the free way of life provided by our government.

The experiences of the ages teach that religiously sensitive persons do not just happen; they are produced and molded through the years as a consequence of the organized efforts of religious institutions. Whatever these institutions are called—a church, a synagogue, a temple, an ethical society, or something else—their collective wisdom, written in their holy books, embodied in their creeds and traditions, and lived out explicitly in the lives of their most devout adherents, would never be available to bless humanity without institutions to preserve and pass on this wisdom to future generations.

Organized religion and the institutions it spawns are essential to the emergence of a spiritual depth needed in our national life. As important as politics is, it is no substitute for, nor a supplement for, the invaluable contribution strong religious institutions make to the lives of persons. In no way is my personal involvement in politics an outlet for frustration over the problems confronting religious institutions. The longer I live, the stronger grows my conviction of the need for effective religious institutions.

I am not involved in politics because I cannot do anything else or enjoy doing anything else. The opposite is closer to the truth; there are so many things I think I could do, maybe not well but at least sufficient to earn a living—and would enjoy doing—that I wish I could live a hundred lives. As a lad, on different occasions, I aspired to be a lawyer, doctor, teacher, minister, coach, and politician. I continue to be fascinated by these vocations, and adult experiences have kindled an interest in banking, architecture, business, and real estate. I am in politics, not by chance or through a process of eliminating all the vocations I do not enjoy, but because I choose to be a politician.

It needs to be said–I am not in politics for the money. I grew up in a family that had few of this world's possessions so I never became accustomed to money and the things money can buy. I suppose I owe my mother more than I realize for instilling in me an attitude toward money that I consider sound. She never had much money and only wanted enough, as she put it many times "to make ends meet."

I am a half century old and during my fifty years have known more people ruined by too much money than destroyed by too little. As a clergyman I have presided over funerals for the wealthy and the poor, and have never once found money capable of bringing back to life the inhabitant of a casket. Money will not make a person happy nor will the absence of it make a person happy, either. Happiness that depends on money for its base is fleeting.

To enter a vocation with money as the basic motivation is unwise. The truly unhappy are those who are trapped in a life they do not enjoy, being required to do things they do not believe in, and forced to face each day with the realization that its labors are really not what they want to be doing. Many find themselves in such circumstances and remain there for one reason—money. Unfortunate are those over whom money has such influence.

Politics is hell on earth if a person involved in it does not believe in it and enjoy it. Great wealth cannot be accumulated honestly in politics but one can, to use my mother's term, "make ends meet." That is enough for those who believe in and enjoy politics.

I am not in politics to acquire power for power's sake. There is something very "heady" about being involved in politics. To participate in making laws or to acquire the legal right to administer the law permits one human to exercise authority over another. From earliest childhood most persons derive pleasure from being in a position of telling others what to do and then seeing them do it. The realization that the possession of power is real and no longer a desired objective can do strange things to people.

I find I must be on watch constantly not to permit whatever political or governmental power I possess to transform me into a tyrant. It matters not at what level of politics and government a person is involved—once power is achieved the possibilities of tyranny are there.

Persons who become involved in politics for selfless reasons to serve others must be especially cautious in administering whatever power they have. It is so easy to delude themselves into thinking that purity of motive removes all possibility of the abuse of power. It does not. Checks on grants of power must always be written into the law to protect the public against those who do not start out to acquire power for power's sake but gradually develop an affection for power that overcomes their rationality.

I am not involved in politics to garner as much fame and prestige as possible. This possibility is akin to the quest of power for power's sake. Fame, prestige, power—they are all cut from the same cloth.

Ministers becoming involved in politics have to be especially careful that they do not get carried away by the pomp of politics. I have always thought that many ministers have large egos. For persons to presume to tell others how to live and to suggest what God's message is, requires at least considerable self-confidence. Once the pastorate is entered and ministers hear how effective their preaching is, how helpful their pastoral calls are, and how proud their parish is of them, they begin to feel (usually subconsciously) that they are unusual. They may come to enjoy the accolades that are poured out upon them.

Consequently, a minister like myself who gets involved in politics is ripe for becoming impressed with the pomp of politics. However, the defeats and bruises one experiences in politics have a leveling influence. I experienced many defeats and bruises in the pastorate, but they were not in the public spotlight like those I have endured in the world of politics.

The temptation is always there, though, to let the clamor of one's ego submerge the worthier reasons for political involvement. Getting oneself out of the way so the real work of life can be done is always a persistent problem.

I am not in politics to prove to myself or family and friends that I can achieve importance. Maybe I am more conscious of this possibility than most. I am the youngest of fourteen children and all my life older brothers and sisters have set the example, shown the way, and reminded me that "my time" would arrive. As a small boy I chafed under their reprimands and told myself that the day would come when I would "prove myself" to them.

Now that I am an adult, rationally I know I do not have to prove myself to my brothers and sisters, many of whom are dead. But psychologically, I may go to my grave trying to prove what really does not have to be proved among those who love and respect one another.

I am not in politics to remake the world and its political institutions after my personal image of what they ought to be. I can recall when I was in my late twenties and early thirties, I thought I had the answer to most problems. I longed to be called to the pastorate of a large church and yearned for election to responsible boards and commissions of my national church denomination. I told myself I had these desires, not because of hunger for fame, prestige, and power, but because I had answers to current problems in our denomination and was capable of successfully applying what I knew.

Today I realize how foolish I was. I no longer believe I have the answers, nor am I so confident of my ability to be successful in the positions to which I am elected or appointed, either in the life of the church or in politics. Increasingly I am convinced that God is not particularly concerned about whether the answers we possess or the activities in which we engage bring permanent solutions to our vexing problems. But I am certain he expects all of us to accept responsible labors and do the best we can with whatever personal equipment nature has endowed us. Frankly, I am relieved to do what I can and leave the rest to God and those who seek to serve him with their lives. To do what I can in politics takes all the energy I possess.

If what I have just discussed helps eliminate reasons why I am not involved in politics, hopefully the following four conclusions as to why I am involved in politics will help point the way to responsible and responsive political participation.

First, I am involved in politics because I enjoy politics. My joy is not shallow. It is derived from political participation in activities that are valuable. I was raised under the auspices of the Protestant work ethic which emphasizes that idol hands are the devil's workshop. For good or for bad, pure idleness has never brought me much enjoyment.

In politics there is little opportunity for idleness. The days begin early and run late into the night and are filled with activity. Almost every day is different from the one before. Opportunities are numerous for contacts with all kinds of people. The rich and the poor, the leading citizens of a community and those from a wide range of ethnic backgrounds, members of a variety of religious faiths, and representatives of as many organizations as exist—all are constituents with whom a politician has involvements. For those who feel variety is the spice of life, politics is a perfect vocation.

My personal inclinations have always led me to a fascination with new experiences. Those new experiences are there by the bundle in politics and I awaken to each day thrilled because I do not know what is going to happen.

Second, I am involved in politics because I genuinely like people, and political involvement provides many opportunities for association with all kinds of people in a vast array of differing situations. Politics is certainly no place for persons who do not like to be around people. In a democracy a politician must win the support of a majority of the people, and if a politician does not genuinely respect the right of people to choose their leaders he or she can never be effective as a politician. I have known politicians who really did not like people but succeeded in hiding their dislike of people from their constituency. After awhile, though, the truth does leak out that they have an anathema toward people. Then their effectiveness is ended.

Politicians have to accept people for what they are even though they may not agree with the positions they take or necessarily respect the substance of their opinions. Politicians always commit a great error when they presume, over a period of time, to substitute their own judgment for that of their constituencies.

A considerable body of literature in political philosophy is devoted to the role of a politician in a democracy—is he to represent his best judgment or the collective wishes of constituents? This question was discussed earlier and there is no need to rehash that discussion. However, I do want to emphasize that over a period of time if a politician is unable to influence his constituency to adopt public policies along lines about which he feels deeply, he is probably unwise to continue in public service. In a democracy, the people deserve to have leaders who are comfortable with the majority's collective philosophy.

To possess such compatibility requires a basic affection for one's constituency. The development of this affection must be based on the genuine affection for people. I suppose I was destined, coming from such a large family, either to like people because I was always surrounded by so many of them or to detest them because I tired of their presence! Thankfully, I came out of my large family background with a genuine liking for people and have found this positive inclination toward persons to be of great benefit in my work as a politician and also in my previous labors as a clergyman.

Third, I am involved in politics because I believe political decisions have a tremendous bearing on people's lives. If one genuinely likes people, he desires the best for them and wants to be involved in activities which help and do not hinder people from gaining the greatest fulfillment in life.

Every day new fields of endeavor are opened to persons, and others closed, by decisions made in governmental bodies at all levels. To recount the number of ways in which government and politics affect the lives of people would require a listing of almost every decision government ever makes. Government expresses the collective will of its constituents. Those who bear the responsibility for speaking and acting in behalf of the total people hold in their hands the earthly fate of many lives.

I was often frustrated in the ministry because I found people needing help I was unable to provide. I was disturbed by many public policies which I felt detrimental to the kind of environment people need in order to lead productive and satisfying lives. It was frustrations such as those which led me to politics. I have not been disappointed in the many opportunities that have been mine in the world of politics to be involved in activities that do have a tremendous bearing on people's lives.

Fourth, I am involved in politics because I believe that the God I worship wants me to serve him by helping people in whatever manner I can. If I have one single ambition in life it is to finish my days on earth knowing that, for the most part, I have done my best to serve God in the manner he desires. I recognize my fallibility and know that when death is just a moment away it will bring to close a life that failed many times to measure up to God's expectations. But I desire that those failures be as few in number as possible.

Every life has something that it values above all else, and that which I value above all else is my firm conviction that the God I worship loves his children and expects his children to love and help each other. I have always taken great comfort in the words of Abraham Lincoln when censored for his unwavering policy in defense of the Union. He provided this answer for his critics: "I am not bound to win, but I am bound to be true. I am not bound to succeed, but I am bound to live up to what light I have. I must stand with anybody that stands right; stand with him while he stands right and part company with him when he goes wrong."[52] This is how I feel about my involvement in politics. I know I will not always win and that failure will be my fate as often as success. Every day I must judge the stands which others take as to whether they are in accord with the values that I hold. If I think their stands are right I must stand with them, and if I think their stands are wrong I must oppose them.

I recognize that the whole thrust of this book has been to emphasize values. I am convinced that a major need confronting all of us today is for a greater emphasis upon values.

I have tried to find that delicate balance between loyalty to my highest values and tolerance for those who hold different values. But the bottom line is this: Persons do what they do because of what they believe. I believe religion is of far more importance in the world of politics than is commonly accepted today. I invite those readers who share this conviction to join in what may be a lonely crusade to obtain a greater mixture of religion and politics in American society. Speak out—politicians need to be heard. God knows and cares about politicians, too, and wants them to lead lives that portray the relevance of religion to politics.

Amen.

Endnotes

Prologue and Chapter 1

1. *The Wall Street Journal,* "Extraordinary Standards," September 23, 1977, p. 20.
2. *Ibid.*
3. From *Hamlet,* Act V, Scene 1.

Chapter 2

4. Merle Miller, *Plain Speaking.* Berkley Publishing Corporation, 1974, p. 56.
5. Joseph Tussman, *The Supreme Court on Church and State,* Oxford University Press, Inc., 1962, p. 256.
6. Bernard M.G. Reardon, ed., *Liberal Protestantism,* London: Adam and Charles Black, 1968, p. 12.
7. John W. Gardner, *Excellence.* Harper & Row, 1961, p. 48.
8. Reinhold Niebuhr, *Moral Man and Immoral Society,* Charles Scribner's Sons, 1960, p. 50.
9. *Ibid.,* p. 81.
10. Gardner, *Excellence,* p. 157.
11. Aristotle, *Politics,* The Great Books Foundation, Chicago, 1948, p. 27.
12. Niebuhr, *Moral Man and Immoral Society,* p. 4.
13. *Ibid.,* p. 9.
14. Carl T. Rowan, " 'Back to God' Ticket," *The Kansas City Times,* July 17, 1976, p. 19c.
15. Gardner, *Excellence,* p. 98.
16. Senator Mark Hatfield, from a speech given at Westminster College, Fulton, Missouri, February 20, 1977.

Chapter 3

17. See Leo Strauss and Joseph Cropsey, *History of Political Philosophy "St. Thomas Aquinas."* Rand, McNally & Co., p. 221.
18. *Ibid.* p. 207.
19. Jimmy Carter, *Why Not the Best?* Broadman, 1977, p. 128.
20. James Q. Wilson, *The Amateur Democrat,* University of Chicago Press, 1962, p. 164.
21. *The Life and Selected Writings of Thomas Jefferson,* edited by Adrianne Koch and William Peden, Random House, Inc., 1944, p. 332.
22. George H. Sabine, *A History of Political Theory,* rev. ed. Holt, Rinehart & Winston, 1950, p. 180.
23. Thomas Sanders, *Protestant Concepts of Church and State.* Doubleday & Company, Inc. 1965, p. 18.
24. Hatfield, Westminster College speech.
25. Doris Kearns, *Lyndon Johnson and the American Dream.* Harper & Row, Publishers, 1976, p. 141.

Chapter 4

26. *Writings of Thomas Jefferson,* p. 466-467.
27. *Ibid.,* p. 460.
28. Kearns, *Lyndon Johnson,* p. 155.
29. Congressional Record, Sept. 28, 1955.
30. Ray W. Wallace, "Live as Free Men," *The Disciple,* September 4, 1977, p. 19.
31. Everett C. Ladd, Jr. " 'Reform' Is Wrecking the U.S. Party System," *Fortune,* November, 1977, p. 178.
32. *Ibid.,* p. 188
33. Wilson, *The Amateur Democrat,* p. 357.
34. Kearns, *Lyndon Johnson,* p. 156.
35. David Broder, *The Party's Over.* Harper & Row, 1971, p. 243.

Chapter 5

36. Carter, *Why Not the Best?* p. 79.
37. *The Wall Street Journal,* June 4, 1976.
38. *Ibid.*
39. Editorial, *The Kansas City Times,* July 30, 1977.
40. Hatfield, *Between a Rock and a Hard Place,* Word Books, 1977, p. 20-21.

Chapter 6

41. From article in *The Washington Post,* copyright 1977; used by permission.
42. Niebuhr, *Moral Man and Immoral Society,* p. 226.
43. Henry David Thoreau, *Walden,* Vail-Ballou Press, 1946, p. 129.

Chapter 7

44. William Barclay, *A Book of Everyday Prayers,* Harper & Row, Publishers, 1959, p. 82.
45. Carter, *Why Not the Best?* p. 139.
46. Niebuhr, *Moral Man and Immoral Society,* p. 156.
47. David Kucharsky, *The Man from Plains–The Mind and Spirit of Jimmy Carter,* Harper & Row, 1977, p. 57-58.
48. Carter, *Why Not the Best?* p. 136.
49. *The Kansas City Times,* July 3, 1976, p. 13c.
50. William E. Simon, *A Time for Truth,* McGraw-Hill Book Company, 1978, p. 216.
51. *Ibid.,* p. 237.

Epilogue

52. Abraham Lincoln, from a speech given in Peoria, Illinois, Oct. 16, 1854.